MARITIME HERITAGE
Newcastle and the River Tyne

HMS Nelson, laid down in September 1906 at Palmer's Hebburn yard .

KEN GROUNDWATER

SILVER LINK PUBLISHING LTD
The Coach House, Garstang Road, St Michael's, Lancashire, PR3 OTG

CONTENTS

© Ken Groundwater & Silver Link Publishing Ltd.

Designed by Barbara Allen/Leading Edge Press & Publishing
Jacket Design by Nigel Harris.

First published in the UK, May 1990

Imagesetting by Ps&Qs, Liverpool and printed in the UK by The Amadeus Press, Huddersfield, Yorkshire.

ISBN 0 947971 44 0

A CIP record is available for this book from the British Library

FRONT COVER: Without doubt one of the most elegant of the Tyne's liners, the *Giulio Cesare* was launched from Swan Hunter & Wigham Richardson's Yard in the autumn of 1921, weighing 21,600 tons. The order from the Navigazione Generale Italiana of Genoa included specifications which would rank her alongside the legendary *Mauretania*, also from Tyneside. Geared turbines drove four screws and the ship had accomodation for 2,870 passengers, some 250 enjoying the luxury of bath and shower facilities, using salt water. She was immediately popular in service on the New York service and by 1932 flew the flag of the Fascist Italian Government. The ship was converted for use as a static restaurant/nightclub at various South African venues; this also proved uneconomic. In 1937, the *Giulio Cesare* came under the control of Lloyd Triestino with more success. In 1942 she became an International Red Cross ship and, after making several journeys of mercy, was bombed by the Allies whilst anchored at Trieste. She was badly damaged and subsequently keeled-over to lie for some time half submerged. Eventually, almost stripped of her finery she was left to founder until her remains were dragged off to the breakers in 1948, a sad fate for a Princess of the seas. *Swan Hunter (SB) Ltd.*

Pride of the Tyne - the RMS Mauretania is seen leaving the place of its birth, attended by a flotilla of steam tugs and amidst much jubilation. Launched on September 20 1906 by the Dowager Duchess of Roxburgh, her keel had been laid in August 1904. Trials took place during 1907. Newcastle was extremely and justly proud of this regal liner. See also page 28/29. *John H. Proud/Courtesy the family of W. Haig Parry.*

INTRODUCTION

THIS book aims to illustrate the changing fortunes of the River Tyne, a river which in shipping terms became internationally conspicuous almost by accident, although the presence of immense local coal reserves provided a solid foundation for its growth development.

Although we are aiming in these pages to illustrate the river's shipping associations its associated commerce is impossible to **ignore** for it spells out clearly how each peripheral industry prospered and gave an army of Tynesiders generations of river-based employment. But in the words of Tyne historian R. W. Johnson:

"....the day of good things is short and the harvest of the Tyne must be reaped quickly, for competition.... began his reign in this land today....."

The river's well-known ship-building career grew from the need to provide quick and cheap transport to carry coal to 12th century London. Why Northern coal? Astonishingly, this was chiefly because it was the only area in England which could provide the resources required for coal transport in the vast quantities needed. This is believed to be our heritage from Norse neighbours, who left in their haste the odd broken longboat for scrutiny and the odd strange word which may be still heard today; 'Geordie.'

Boats were the best way of transporting the north east's coal, for the turnpike roads of England hadn't reached the standards needed to facilitate the constant passage and hammering inflicted by coal carts. At this time, the coming of 'ways-of-rail'

A quite superb Tyne view on April 20 1965 shows *British Craftsman* going to sea, under tow, past the staiths at Hayhole Point. In the foreground awaiting a berth is the collier John Orwell Phillips. This ship was built on the Wear, by Pickersgill & Sons, in 1955 and served the North Thames Gas Board (making many visits to the Tyne) until her sale to Panamanian interests in 1968. *South Shields Gazette.*

was a long time away. The pit-owners therefore had no choice but to send boats to London and thus the Tyne collier soon choked the Pool of London with all the resemblance of a black-armada !

The Monks at Tynemouth who went down to the beach 'Haven' below their priory (see final river-map) in the 12th century to pick 'sea-cole' needed Royal Assent to do so, but their back-yard beach business had begun. Development was steady

4

from this point and the large collier fleet eventually based in the North-East was the biggest single group of co-ordinated shipping ever seen around our shores. Londoners found the produce from the Northern coalfield ideal for their uses.

The only physical restraint to the continuous supply of the black mineral was the receding 'coal-line.' The essentially 'open-cast' coal-picking operation moved further and further from the shore and supply inevitably slowed in consequence. Early railways, in the form of wooden wagon guides, thereafter became a priority. Still, for almost 100 years, horses hauled crude chaldron wagons down the mud paths to the awaiting ships. These sea-going ships, in turn unable to navigate the still shallow Tyne, had eventually to await at the River's mouth for smaller craft to bring the minerals down to them.

Although it may seem odd to introduce a maritime subject by dwelling upon coal-trade development, it was the developing need to move large sea-going ships up the river, closer to the coal sources, that prompted both river improvements and the burgeoning shipping industry.

In his book *The Making of the Tyne*, R.W. Johnson paints a picture of an early river-scene and its limitations that today might be hard to believe :

"It was a tortuous, shallow stream, full of sandbanks and eccentric eddies, which at Newcastle men might ford at low tide. It wended its peaceful course from the junction of the North and South Tyne above Hexham through a charming valley.......meandering by Stephenson's lonely cottage near Wylam, between the drooping willows of Ryton, doubling round Newburnhaugh and stealing with quickened force on either side of the King's Meadow, the rustic river sped on untrammelled and unstained 'till its waters darkened under the shadow of Newcastle Town. But even here, though deeper of hue and enslaved to the service of man, its wayward course was unfettered still. The Tyne, over what was then its navigable reach, twisted, turned, and expanded, now rushing with impetuous haste past the mid-stream projection of Bill Point.....stretching its expanse over the marshes of Jarrow Slake, only to gather fresh force for the sweep around Whitehill Point and the final charge through the "narrows" at Shields into the broad sea beyond........."

The Tyne then was still unsuited to the increasing demands of the coal industry, for as Johnson went on to add, the natural blessing of coal did not extend to the natural shape of the river. Nevertheless, from as early as

Above: Newcastle and Gateshead quayside. Also prominent are Newcastle's Central Station and the bridges. At the quay berths is an Ellerman Line boat with numerous small trawlers laid up beyond the Ouseburn area. The apparent 'chaos' in the foreground is the Elswick Gas Works, Associated Lead, and the remains of Richardson's Tannery. River effluent can be seen to be very much a problem associated with this 1960s scene. *University of Newcastle.*

1620, coal was passing from the upper-reaches in early keel boats under the guidance of men who were learning about sand-bank shoals that shifted with every tide! They were already experienced in night navigation by dim lights in foggy Novembers and they were particularly adept at taking sudden avoiding action at Shields upon sight of larger vessels looming out of the fog on the Tyne.

In these conditions the river's working life rolled on for another 200 years or so and may never have altered had it not been for the dogged persistence of liberal-thinking and fearless campaigners. These people, for their sins, were persecuted and bribed to be quiet, but they would not be silent and set about to reveal :

"..the illegal oppresions and arbitrary exactions barbourous murthers, practised and committed by the magistrates of Newcastle, both upon their neighbours and the free people of this nation........."

The constrictions upon free-trading upon the river continued, accompanied by rumblings of discontent. In 1800, the campaigners were narrowly acquitted for obstruction at the Northumberland Assizes. Still, it took another 50 years of haggling before the River Tyne Improvement Act took effect and opened the way to prosperity via the spirit of free enterprise. Development followed quickly as if a flood-tide had released a mass of energy and enthusiasm and the modern river shape that we find today finally took form. Today, of course, the forest of masts common in the late 19th century has gone, together with the the steep-sided steel cargo holds of the 1930s, also the hustling 'flat-iron' colliers of the 1940s and 1950s. Nevertheless, the Tyne still retains a unique atmosphere, with its high-sided banks, where pidgeon-lofts sit comfortably between the serried rows of cranes and landscaped industrial swathes.

To understand just a little of the

pride felt by local people when the river was producing its first 'giant machines' let us hear some contempory waxings. Here, Charleton is recounting the maritime aspects as seen from a 'view' at 1883.

"...going back to 1750 we find great excitement ...on the occasion of the launch of the *Russell* from Mr. Headlam's yard. She was (we are to believe) a fine vessel capable of carrying 30 keels of coal and the largest ship built on the river. Then in 1753, we read how the *Experiment*, built by subscribers to a West Indian trade, came back from her first

Below: This aerial view encompasses the area shown on Maps E and E1. It looks down to the once busy and recently revitalised Albert Edward Dock. The staiths have been cut back and timber wagons stand idle whilst a large ship stands across the river, at Readhead's yard, adjacent to the Tyne Dock Lock gates. Views like this merit close study...much has now gone forever!
University of Newcastle.

voyage... ...with a cargo of sugar, rum, and coffee in return for the commodities of Newcastle."

He goes on: "Its banks from Scotswood to the sea resound with the din of the riveters' hammer. Shipyards are to be seen at every bend and on both sides....their number is rapidly increasing. The produce of the Tyne in 1882 was 133 steamers and 7 sailing vessels.........it is pleasant to look upon... these labours, and to see that they have made the Tyne of the present day one of the chief ports of Gt. Britain. During 1881...its 11,363 vessels to and from foreign countries....came second only to London—Liverpool being third. In the coasting trade, the Tyne is 6th in the list, with 11,032 vessels.......'

Charleton would certainly be astounded by the much quieter Tyne of today!

So, how shall we embark on our nostalgic journey along this historic waterway? We first of all start by looking at the upper industries from the mouth of the Derwent, before sailing downstream through the industrial corridor lining Scotswood and Dunston, to the famous bridges which have become the city's hallmark. Our river maps indicate industrial sites and whilst they do not represent their exact size in terms of scale they are included to convey their presence in relation to river activity. We have not attempted to show all river-side industry at the turn of the century as change was constant and the map for 1895 had totally changed by 1914. We apologise, therefore, if you fail to identify your great Grandfather's glue factory, or a distant relative's alkali works! Each section is accompanied by a synopsis of the river's main features, before the picture coverage starts. It is recommended that the map description is read before starting to examine the illustrations. The industrial expansion was entwined with the presence of an already highly developed system of railways leading, in most cases down to the banks of the river. Communications were never a problem in this respect, although the high banks and tiered construction of some of the factories posed transfer problems.

Many of the smaller early shipyards, especially in the South Shields area are difficult to 'pin down' precisely, for surviving records don't always include their precise geographical locations. But at least we know early owners names, thanks,in particular to the fine exhaustive research undertaken by Miss Amy Flagg and her book, mentioned in the bibliography. More recently, an extensive 'dig' just behind the Quayside area at Newcastle, led by the energetic Colm O'Brien, has proved of inestimable value in determining the activities of medieval riverside activities and confirmed that early boat-building did, in fact take place during charcoal-burning industrial beginnings.

We very much hope that younger generations of Tynesiders will at least try to understand their unique heritage. The 1990s sees the derelict, post-industrial dock wastelands and silted quays reawakening as the locations of dream homes of the upwardly-mobile. Everybody, it seems, wants a waterside view and their own boat-mooring. Such developments are transforming riverside Newcastle: quayside developements are bringing new office space whilst the St Peter's basin development of 281 homes will bring people back into the city centre. In spite of all this new-found hype, let us not forget our roots!

Ken Groundwater,
Low Fell,
Gateshead,
April 1990.

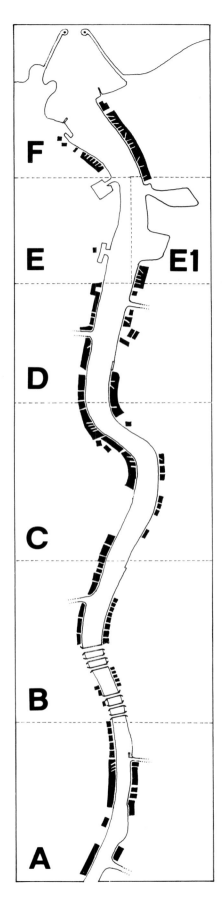

Right: A sketch map of the Tyne, from Scotswood to the river's mouth, indicating our areas of coverage, chapter by chapter, as we move downriver.

Section A

SCOTSWOOD TO REDHEUGH

IN 1620, this stretch of river boasted the most peaceful of river settings. Even so, the shallow Tyne, as it swirled around the three-island mid-river group off Elswick, was collecting coal traces from the opposite shore, which had trickled down the Team from this country's first staith-like structure.

By 1820, industry had arrived and the rural setting was broken by flecks of smoke rising from early factories. By 1893, it was incomprehensible to the onlooker that nature's fair-hand had ever touched this shore-line. Everywhere, smoke lay a thick rich pattern, the river roads were constantly in turmoil; boats of all shapes and sizes jostled for key positions off the new North Eastern Railway staiths; Elswick echoed to a barrage of sound as Armstrong's men beat iron plates into formidable fighting machines......the landscape here would never be quite the same again.

But our maritime review begins higher upstream, at Scotswood, where, less than a mile from the Elswick Works, men waded with salmon-nets and children swam for fun. It was along this shore in the old parish of Whickham, that industrial Tyneside started life. It is an appropriate place to begin our journey down the 'coaly' Tyne. On the Whickham shore (Dunston) the saltmarshes had become the home for the gas-works and coke-ovens. Roads and rails entwined and the river became suddenly claustrophobic as

urban housing closed-in. Map A illustrates the first part of our journey down the River Tyne. Newburn is significant for two reasons. Firstly, the last Tyne wherries lay here on the mud-banks, seen at low-tide, and were destroyed just before their importance became recognised (see page 11). Also, the stretch of river between the two Stella Power Stations is still remembered by local people as the 'Cromwell' crossing, recalling the time the Scots army crossed here as allies to the Great Protector.

Travelling first first along the south bank, after Scotswood Bridge was the first of the many staiths, beginning with Blaydon Main Staith. Alongside was Derwenthaugh Staiths, where the produce of the Consett area pits would arrive at the river, via the Garesfield and Chopwell sorting sidings. Today, the remnant of the eastern-arm jetty is the base of a marina.

Next is the Derwent rivermouth and the location of early iron works, paper mills and fire-brick works, which all utilised the river for power as well as for navigation, for it was within the tidal-limit. Over the Derwent is the Delta Iron Works. Dating back to the late 18th century, it supplied Nelson's navy with grappling-irons, grape-shot and canon. The abortive West Dunston Staiths (perhaps the biggest mistake made by the NER) stand next adjacent to their sidings....today swept away by coach-parks serving instead the Metro Shopping Centre. Central to our first area of review is Dunston power station, built between 1931 and 1933 and served by both wharf and rail sidings. This closed in 1981 and is also an area ear-marked for car park development. The next industry was Clayton & Davie, where many fine old ships and steam-engines ended their days; this site, now abandoned, is also an industrial embarrassment for the

Above: Dunston Staiths attracted colliers and coasters from almost every maritime country. On September 5 1977, *MV Lindo*, built in 1972 in the Brodrene Lothe Yard (Sweden) is an example of the modern, versatile general cargo ship which became the norm with the gradual disappearance of the CEGB 'flat-irons' in the 1970s. For her multi-purpose role she has an ice-strengthened hull, five winches and, with the callsign LJXK, sailed under the Norwegian Flag to the orders of Paal Wilson & Co. On this occasion, her load comprised pitch (a tar-like bi-product of coke) which had perhaps surprisingly been brought by rail from Kilnmarsh, Yorkshire, due to a shortfall locally. Because of this lightweight cargo, *Lindo* would call in at Jarrow for ballasting before her long journey (33 days) to British Columbia, via the Panama Canal. *Ken Groundwater.*

Metro-centre developers.

After Dunston Engine Works we pass the remnants of the Co-op Flour Mills. This surviving 'listed' building is included within the framework of the Garden Festival, together with stories relating to its history. Next we pass the massive Dunston Staiths.....built out into the river by the fiercely competitive NER. The site has a lineage dating back to 1620 and for the fascinating life-story of its evolution I recommend *Coal to Chrysanthemums*, to be published by the Portcullis Press. Coming to the southern limit of the Map A area, it only remains to look towards the sky, before we are eclipsed by the new Redheugh Bridge, and visually compare its fine effortless lines with the heavily constructed bridges of an earlier era.

Along the northern bank, the present Scotswood Bridge may be seen to mark the beginning of maritime industries. The current modern bridge replaced the one shown on page 11. This previous elegant and still much-beloved Chain Suspension Bridge was built in 1831 and is seen being dismantled in 1967.....a victim of modern day traffic. Beyond this point and once stretching as far as the eye could see, were the long thin Armstrong works, perhaps the greatest Tyneside success story of the 19th century. Dating from 1847 and with interests in hydraulic machinery the company eventually became an armaments business at the time of the Crimean War. It subsequently flourished as a result of major Government orders for warships. The Works will be remembered by those with a naval interest for the many 'Elswick Cruisers' launched before the turn of the century. The site however became one of two under the Armstrong, Mitchell amalgamation; the other shipbuilding site at Walker became, from 1882, the building location for merchantmen and lighter warships. Perhaps best remembered from the Elswick stable is *HMS Victoria*, launched in 1887, (see page 12) packing 10,470 tons within 363 feet and launched at a slew. At the time, she was to be principal flagship of the Mediterranean Fleet under Admiral Sir George Tyron. Her fate accompanies the caption.

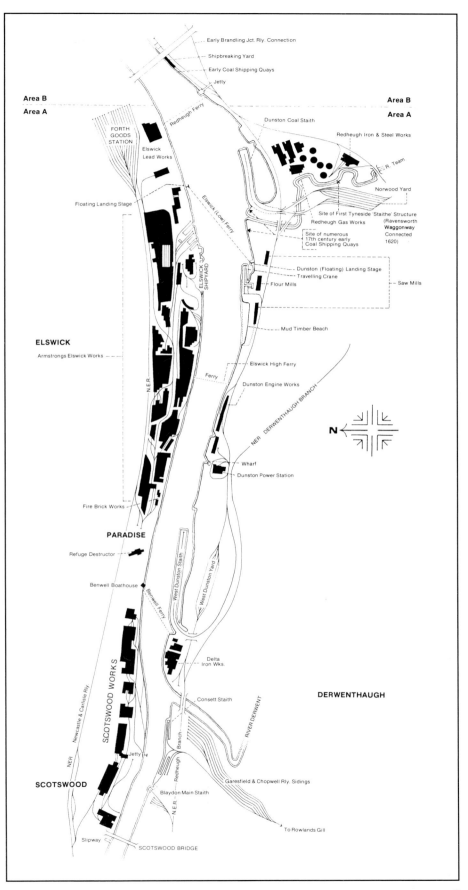

Right: A general view of the 1893-vintage staiths at Dunston showing the base of the inner area staith, removed in 1970 following closure. This was mainly due to silting of the inner basin with consequent high dredging costs and a preference to use the stronger-built river side staith. The clear division between the two staiths illustrates how the 'new' side had been annexed onto the more solid riverside berth, which ceased operations in 1980. *Ken Groundwater.*

Below: Another view of Dunston Staiths taken on November 13 1977. The mooring posts in the foreground were again high in the water in 1990 following dredging of the basin area for National Garden Festival water bus clearance. The bus will berth at the point from which this photograph was taken. *Trevor Ermel.*

Above: A classic Tyneside scene at Dunston Staiths, where coal was loaded aboard ship. Built by S.P. Austin & Son Ltd (Sunderland) as Yard No 409, *Brunswick Wharf* was completed in 1951 to join her many sisters in the fleet of the British Electricity Authorities, London. In 1954 her ownership became the CEA and in 1959, after this photograph was taken, she displayed the CEGB logo on her funnel. She is shown at 7/8 berth in the 'new' inside basin at Dunston. The ship is high in the water and has recently berthed prior to loading 2,000 tons of coal. These boats, with their low profile and hinged funnels, would easily make the journey to the power stations of the Thames in two days. Her days as a collier ended in 1974 but she survives today as a cement storage hulk at Oslo, Norway. *John Johnson.*

Right: Dunston Staiths at work in 1957. This interesting view shows the essence of this traditional Tyne business, which dates back to the 17th century. This view shows the Central Electricity Authority boat *Sir Leonard Pearce* receiving a coal load from spouts 3/4 whilst at 5/6 stands the MV *Marius Neilsen*, also busy taking coke from the adjacent Norwood Works. 'Sir Leonard' was named after the Engineer in Chief of Battersea Power Station, who was knighted in 1935. The vessel was built by the Burntisland Shipbuilding Company in 1941 for the London Power Company. She survived only another three years before being scrapped at Sunderland. *Marius Neilsen* was a much younger ship, of 1954, and was named after a Danish shipping agent. She was sold in 1970 to the Fos Shipping Company and as *Poliere* survived only a matter of weeks when she was wrecked at the Kettle Rock off Tresco Isles (off the Scillies) whilst sailing from Foyness to Gdynia, in Poland. Her change of name apparently brought her no luck. *John Johnson.*

Left: Strictly speaking, this is outside the area of our remit, but this view of traditional Tyne wherries has too much local maritime interest to be excluded. Once a common sight everywhere on the river, these last examples lay at Newburn near Cromwells Crossing, rotting from about 1959 to 1970. They were thrown together for the sake of tidying the environment at a time when authorities did not fully appreciate the full importance of their own 'back yard' inheritance. Steps to save them had been initiated when the news arrived that they had been removed by a scrapdealer working to contract. They would have dated back to the turn of the century but their lineage and clinker construction go back a lot further.... to the Norsemen. *University of Newcastle.*

Below right. Not strictly of maritime importance but an important marker of heavy industry along the banks of the Tyne was the Chain Bridge at Scotswood, built in 1831 by John Green. It was an aesthetically pleasing construction and survived until 1967 when increasingly heavy traffic proved to be too much of a burden for its relatively lightweight construction. Vickers' Elswick works stretched from here to a point almost adjacent to the Redheugh Bridge...and the limit of Map 'A'. *John Johnson.*

Above: Moored between Elswick and Dunston in April 1946 is war casualty SS *Harpagus*. The ship was waiting in the queue for a berth at Swan Hunter's yard, behind more urgent wartime naval repair jobs. Eventually to be re-joined with a brand new bow section, she later became the *Treworlas* of the Hains Fleet and ended her days at Briton Ferry in September 1960. The ship broke in two on August 19 1944, when she was within yards of her destination, Arromanches, on a voyage from Southend, carrying military stores. The ship struck a mine and her fore-part quickly sank, leaving the stern section afloat, to be towed firstly to Southampton and then the Tyne, where she arrived in December 1944. *Laurence Dunn.*

Above: After fitting-out, HMS *Victoria* **carefully** makes her way to sea for trials. Almost all Tyneside turned out to see her squeeze through the Swing Bridge gap. *Victoria* , seen here coming down river from Elswick Works in April 1888, has just passed under the Redheugh Bridge and is approaching the swing bridge. She made a fine stirring sight. *Newcastle Central Library.*

Left. A stern view of the battleship HMS *Victoria,* whilst on her trials off the Tyne on 7th April 1888. She was still without her main mast and much armament. The ornate crest on her stern and the banner scroll displaying her name are all traits of Victorian warship design. She went to serve in the Mediterranean Fleet and became the principal flagship under Admiral Sir George Tyron. However her illustrious career was cut short on the afternoon of June 22 1893 whilst on manoeuvres off Tripoli. The Admiral ordered the fleet to reverse direction by turning the two groups of ships, sailing alongside each other, inward. *Victoria,* leading the starboard group, was turning correctly when HMS *Camperdown,* unable to turn sharply enough, buried her ram in *Victoria's* hull. She settled rapidly and sank within minutes, taking with her 328 officers and men; a terrible tragedy. *John H. Proud/Courtesy the family of W. Haig Parry.*

A 1959 riverfront scene at Dunston. This location is now in the midst of the redeveloped National Garden festival site. The picture shows the bulk of the CWS flour mills and a small portion of the adjacent (former) timber pond area to the right. The mill was the first ferro-concrete construction on this scale on Tyneside in 1891; it had a long, well-dredged frontage. The coaster *Moray Firth* is discharging grain at the 'spiders legs' suction pipes. Various Port of Tyne buoys dot the river around two large concrete barges - another once-common sight on the river. *Ken Groundwater.*

REDHEUGH BRIDGE, NEWCASTLE.

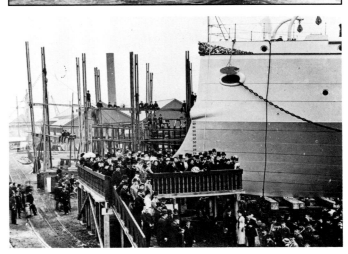

Above: Tyneside in 1895 and the first Redheugh Bridge is seen as constructed by Thomas Bouch (of Tay Bridge notoriety) in 1870. It lasted only six more years before being completely rebuilt. Today, a new bridge constructed in 1983 has succeeded the replacement. Only Stephenson's High Level Bridge and Armstrong's swing bridge can be seen beyond.....the King Edward Bridge was yet to be built (in 1906). Here, at the eastern limit of Map A's coverage, we see a river with a broad shore left undredged to allow the keels and wherries to stand on this hard shoulder. The wherry *George Hope* is receiving coals from a primitive wagon shoot. Other similar examples may be seen further along the quay. In the river, the steam paddle tug *William & John* leads two large wherries and three smaller examples up river to coal spouts, possibly at Lemington. The tug is said to date back to an early South Shields yard owned by James Evans *Auty Collection/Newcastle City Library.*

Left, upper: A likely successor to *William & John* would have been the *Washington* of 1870. Built by Readhead and Softley for John Dry Steam Tugs (Redhead & Dry from the 1930s). *Washington* was bought by France Fenwick and is seen here in a busy lower river scene on the April 26 1939. She survived the Second World War to be broken up at Kings Yard at Redheugh. On the left is a Ropner tramp steamer the *Ainderby,* and to the right, the *Tynemouth* on a 'Ha'penny' ferry run between the two 'Shields'. *South Shields Library*

Left, lower: A launch view of an Elswick Cruiser. The ram bow, of the sort that did so much damage to *HMS Victoria* (see page 12), is clearly evident. The identity of the vessel is unknown. *South Shields Library.*

Right: This aerial photo from 1976 shows the Gateshead Garden Festival Maritime area at Dunston. On the river front on the right are the remains of the Co-op grain silos. The staith at Dunston leads the eye back to the Norwood sidings and around the curve to join the railway leading from Dunston towards Newcastle and the south. The decaying riverfront became totally derelict when the staiths at Dunston ceased working in 1980, the site becoming a prime area for an injection of new life; it earned its enterprise zone status shortly afterwards. Another industrial scar was left as a derelict reminder of busier times past when Norwood Coke Works (extreme middle left) closed in the early 1980s. It is hoped that the various Garden Festival constructions will leave this once heavily industrialised river front revitalised in a new and more permanent way. *University of Newcastle.*

Below right: We are looking down here on the very birthplace of industrial Tyneside. Although much had been cleared by 1970, the vast sprawling line of factories along the northern riverbank show the extent of the once mighty Armstrong Empire, where British and foreign navies were built. Now, no evidence remains of their slipways. At the very top, and behind the Associated Lead Works, is the extensive Forth Goods sidings leading the eye into Newcastle Central station. On the southern bank we see the indent of an early timber pond alongside the reclaimed land of Palmer Halls timber yard. Next comes the Co-op flour mill complex before the staiths swing out into the river. The staiths hinterland includes the badly contaminated Redheugh Coke Works ground, today covered by a capillary action blanket to accommodate a platform for our Garden Festival site. *University of Newcastle.*

Section B

THE BRIDGES TO ST PETERS

THIS area includes both Newcastle and Gateshead quaysides. The first bridge to span the Tyne ravine is said to have been the the Roman Bridge of 120 AD. It was possible – but only just – to negotiate the bridge by rowing boat at high tide. The second, medieval bridge of 1250 encouraged more movements below it, and consequently lasted until 1775 having seen hundreds of 'keels' come and go to the coal-rich banks upstream. Today we have a bridge every few hundred yards and the first encountered along our way is the new (1983) Redheugh

bridge. We next pass under the King Edward bridge of 1906 (rail only) and almost immediately pass beneath the Metro bridge; again this is rail only for rapid transit 'trams'.

The remaining bridges, passed in quick succession, are the earlier group of High Level, Swing and Tyne Bridges, certainly the historical high-point, bearing in mind that each example celebrated unique engineering techniques that were in their time wonders of the world. The swing bridge is perhaps the most remarkable in its early application of the hydraulic concept. The Swing

Above: The main bridge crossing area is clearly illustrated in this view showing Newcastle & Gateshead's waterfront area, in 1976. Reference to Map B (page 16) will help identify main river features. Quayside warehouse sheds are at the very top of the scene. The railway 'circle' formed by the High Level and the King Edward Bridges has a toy train like quality! Between these today is the more recent *Metro* Bridge. The Redheugh Bridge shown is the rebuild of Bouch's first attempt. Today it is different again, following the opening of the Mott, Hay & Anderson design structure in 1983. *University of Newcastle.*

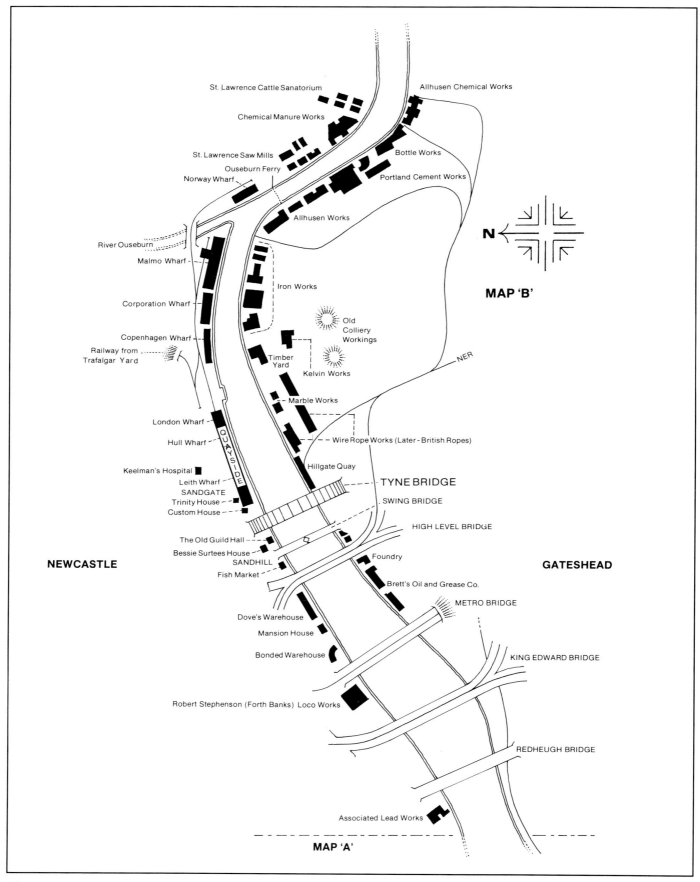

St. Lawrence Cattle Sanatorium

Chemical Manure Works

Allhusen Chemical Works

St. Lawrence Saw Mills

Ouseburn Ferry

Norway Wharf

Bottle Works

Portland Cement Works

Allhusen Works

River Ouseburn

Malmo Wharf

N

MAP 'B'

Iron Works

Corporation Wharf

Old Colliery Workings

Copenhagen Wharf

NER

Railway from Trafalgar Yard

Timber Yard

Kelvin Works

Marble Works

London Wharf

Hull Wharf

QUAYSIDE

Wire Rope Works (Later - British Ropes)

Keelman's Hospital

Hillgate Quay

Leith Wharf

TYNE BRIDGE

SANDGATE

SWING BRIDGE

Trinity House

Custom House

HIGH LEVEL BRIDGE

NEWCASTLE

The Old Guild Hall

Bessie Surtees House

SANDHILL

Fish Market

Foundry

Brett's Oil and Grease Co.

GATESHEAD

METRO BRIDGE

Dove's Warehouse

Mansion House

Bonded Warehouse

KING EDWARD BRIDGE

Robert Stephenson (Forth Banks) Loco Works

REDHEUGH BRIDGE

Associated Lead Works

MAP 'A'

Bridge wasn't cheap and it was not until 1893, with the constant comings and goings to the busy (new) staiths at Dunston that toll-payments quickly totted-up. It was required to 'swing' almost hourly, night and day and was a great attraction to dads and children! In its busiest year, and a 'peak' for coal shipments at Dunston, 1924, 6,000 ships with a net tonnage of 6,327,847 passed. Today, with the Tyne's revived interest, demonstration 'swings' are frequently arranged.

Moving on to the quayside area, we come to the traditional heartland of trading. Excavations by the University have recently revealed that early shipbuilding went on, at the original shore-line, perhaps 50 metres back from the current quay-edge. The most important maritime heritage left to future generations is the Trinity House, the traditional home of the Master-Mariners of Newcastle. Its roots go back to the year of incorporation as a Guild in 1505, when its responsibilities covered light-houses, buoys and (the eventual source of much complaint) control and regulation of the hundreds of river and sea pilots. The implementation of a separate 'Tyne Pilotage Board' in 1865 gave the service a dedicated administrative body which today handles the business of the remaining dozen river-pilots and their two operational boats. Trinity House is open to the public and is a 'must' for shipping enthusiasts, as is the excellent collection in the maritime section of the Museum of Science and Engineering in Blandford Street Newcastle.

Over the years, the quayside has hosted many different types of vessels at its 26 berths. A common landing stage nearby is still today used as the embarkation point for river trips. Along the Quay were, until quite recently, berths dedicated to the various trading companies, such as the Tyne-Tees Shipping Company, which also had a considerable area across at Hillgate Quay. Further around the curve, beyond the Ouseburn mouth, was the regular berthing location for the 'butter-boats' remembered perhaps by older readers. The Danish boats, filled with butter-barrels, and displaying the twin horn legend, were often a daily sight and the barrels were a great source of firewood for small boys wishing to boost their pocket-money.

The Tyne was generally dredged to a depth of 30ft below low water (ordinary tides) and total quay area, at the end of the 1930s extended to 2,000ft. In 1934, the river boasted an incredible 60 regular weekly foreign 'steamship' services. We haven't the space to list them all, but each Saturday there was a sailing to Antwerp with the Tyne-Tees SS Company. Also on Saturdays (during the Summer months) you could leave for Arendal, aboard the ships of the Det Bergenske Dampskibsselskab. Bordeaux was serviced once weekly by the General Steam Navigation Company, whilst Corunna (as traffic demanded) was served by MacAndrew Line vessels. Istanbul was surprisingly connected by three operators, giving a roughly

Above: In April 1960, the SS *Winga* is passing upstream through the swing bridge provided to give access to the staiths at Dunston. The ship was built in 1957 by Alex Hall for Glen & Company, Glasgow. Renamed *Radient* in 1967, she sailed the seas for another 11 years before sinking in Bombay Harbour, after a collision. The Quayside is typically busy with large Scandinavian vessels at the 'common' Quay area. *John Johnson.*

fortnightly service from Newcastle Quay ! There was a further service to Istanbul, via Bremen, and another via Hull and one direct by way of the Westcott & Laurance Line Ltd. It seems difficult to believe today!

To the east end of Hillgate Quay, on the Gateshead side was the shore-based RNVR HMS *Calliope*. The first vessel used was an old corvette dating from 1885; she went to the shipbreakers in 1951. In 1952 the sloop, *Falmouth* was renamed *Calliope* and replaced the corvette.

Our photograph on page 19 shows her fate. Further to the east, the early Marble Works on our map was replaced in 1949 by the impressive Rank Baltic Flour Mill. Today, the mill and the adjacent animal food factory have been demolished, leaving a huge silo as a reminder of the days when 20,000 ton merchantmen would tie-up alongside. There is so much in this half-mile of maritime interest, from Redheugh through to Sandgate, that it only remains for us to conjure up images via our river pictures.

Right: The September evening light catches WD (Westminster Dredging) *Waterway* making her way up river, around 1960, between the King Edward and Redheugh Bridges. Beyond is the remains of Kings shipbreakers yard with cranes standing idle. The building adjacent marks the spot of an early railway-sponsored ferry connecting Redheugh Station with Elswick. This area is now landscaped in conjunction with the 1990 National Garden Festival. *John Johnson.*

Above: An "after the storm" air pervades this lovely classic scene showing the ancient Quayside. From here we look up river via the five bridges of the day, circa 1964. *John Johnson.*

Below: Sylvia Steel, one of the WRN permanent staff at the RNR shore establishment at Gateshead, watches her former training ship HMS *Calliope* being towed away to the breakers yard of Hughes Bolckows at Blyth on the April 30 1968. *Calliope* was actually the 1,000 ton sloop *Falmouth*. Launched at Devonport dockyard in 1951, she took on her training ship role in January 1952 but by the mid-1960s she became a river eyesore as her age began to tell. She was the sixth RN vessel to carry the name. The third (built in 1884) survived a notorious hurricane at Apia to survive until 1951! *South Shields Gazette.*

Left: In the 1970s, the devaluation of the pound encouraged the Scandinavians to do their shopping in this country. This scene, in November 1975, although at a time of North Sea storms, is falsely attributed to the bad weather: the truth was that the crews were all shopping along Northumberland Street, buying their 'cheaper' Christmas presents. This is the nearest the Quayside recently came to the forest of masts well-known up to the 1920s. *South Shields Gazette*

SS. HIGHLANDER
1,215 Tons Gross.

ss. Highlander sails from Aberdeen to Newcastle and Hull every Saturday returning from Hull every Wednesday and from Newcastle every Thursday.

ABERDEEN, NEWCASTLE & HULL STEAM CO. LTD.,
79 REGENT QUAY, ABERDEEN.

Telephone: 5591.   Telegrams: "Abercastle."

Left: Built in 1916 with a gross tonnage of 1,202, the *Highlander* was built by Caledon for the Aberdeen, Newcastle & Hull Steam Company Ltd. This most popular and well-known vessel at Newcastle between the wars docked at Newcastle Quay early Sunday and discharged cattle, sheep and Shetland ponies in time for the Sunday morning market, which still operates in 1990. The rest of the cargo was discharged on the Monday. During Summer months, she ran cruises either to the Farne Islands or Scarborough. The return fare (you couldn't land) was six shillings for adults and three shillings for children. She was acquired by the North of Scotland, Orkney & Shetland Shipping Company in 1939 and she destroyed two enemy aircraft **on** August 1 1940, one landing on her poop! Having been renamed *St Catherine,* she was sunk in an air attack on November 14 1940. *South Shields Libraries.*

Right: In the days before mass containerisation of cargo, *Newcastle Clipper* discharges boxed Israeli oranges at Newcastle Quayside January 29 1974. The clipper was built on the River Tees at Smiths Docks for the Rockhampton Shipping Co. of Glasgow. Looking at a picture like this, it is easy to see why pilferage could be very easy! *Port of Tyne Authority.*

Above: Along the new quay extension of the 1930s, the six-ton Stothert & Pitt dockside cranes enabled quicker cargo discharge. This quayside however was losing out as the commercial heartland of Tyneside to deeper water facilities downriver in the Howdon/Albert Edward areas. Here, under the surveillance of a Port of Tyne manager, a British gypsum lorry from Carlisle loads sacks, whilst sisal (a fibrous product, made from leaves, used in rope manufacture) also comes off for temporary storage before its journey into a Gateshead rope-works. *John Johnson.*

Right: The *Crusader,* on charter to T. & J. Harrison of Liverpool, discharges her casks of resin near to St. Lawrence's whilst stevedores and lorries of the day (a Commer and an AEC's) form a vignette of the early 1960s. Much interesting detail abounds concerning a past way of work. Containerisation and the revolution in handling has resulted in dock-workers like this being something of a rarity along the Tyne today. *John Johnson.*

Left: A splendid view in a rope factory at Wallsend as a warehouseman surveys his stock of brand new rope, seemingly including everything from washing lines to ships hawsers! *University of Newcastle.*

Above: Bales of sisal are put into warehouse storage in the 50s, This commodity, bound for one of the many British Ropes factories that lined the river, would reappear as traditional rope of all sizes. Tyneside was (and still is) the rope-making capital of the north; today the industry is concentrated in the Willington Quay Gut area. *Port of Tyne Authority.*

Below: The hired *Magnus* II lowers an accommodation module for an oil platform into a boat specially modified for the role. Taken on October 10 1974, this view shows the empty riverside berth beyond and is an indication of how oil module work was to eventually dominate the river.... thankfully finding much needed work for ex-shipyard men. *Port of Tyne Authority.*

Above: The *Craftsman*, built by Doxfords in 1972 (10,220tons) on a rare return visit to a North East port in the late 1970s whilst on a heavy lift mission. The ship's heavy lift derricks are preparing to take the strain of 90 tons of machinery at Newcastle Quay. The *Craftsman*, owned by the Charente SS Company was managed by T.& J.Harrison, being registered in Liverpool. She could generate 16,000 bhp from her two Sulzer diesels. *Port of Tyne Authority.*

Below: The 'new' deep water berths at the Newcastle Quay extension proved popular at least up to the 1970s. Here, *Aramaic* (Shaw Saville & Albion Line) once an irregular Tyne visitor, off-loads adjacent to the *Warkworth,* further down river, at the Spillers Wharf in about 1950. The *Warkworth,* until quite recently, would take passengers to Port Churchill during the Summer months only - for holiday makers with plenty of time to spare! Note the old 1920s and 1930s built 'lighters' plying around the hulls of the bigger ships. Behind, the serried rows of working class houses stretch beyond Byker to Heaton. Spillers Tyne Mill built in 1936 - then the largest in Europe - was capable of holding a total of 250,000 tons of grain. This quayside extension in the 1920s increased capacity to 24 berths. *Port of Tyne Authority.*

Above: This fine view of the Norwegian and Danish Quays evokes images of the busy days, when not a single berth would be free and more coasters and tramp ships would be tethered to the buoys. Here, *Olivian Coast* and *Frisian Coast* are at the 'Butter-boat' wharf, whilst beyond is the *Exedene.* At Spillers, with grain, is Ellerman Line's *City of Durban* with its distinctive funnel. Of the four boats in this 1962 picture the *Frisian Coast* dated back to 1937. She held this name from 1946 to 1967 when she became the *Agia Eleni. City of Durban* went on to become the *Mediterranean Dolphin* under Greek interests. *John Johnson.*

Above: A recently acquired war prize, the *Empire Conifer* slips downstream under the doubtless expert eyes of three schoolboys. The *Empire Conifer* started life at Emden in 1935 as the *Adrian* but was ceded to Britain after the war and came under the management of the Tyne Tees Shipping Company. In 1947 she was sold to Australian interests. This is an evocative quayside view of a still war-weary 'grey-coated' Tyneside. *University of Newcastle.*

Section C
ST PETERS TO LOW WALKER

IN 1880, the local historian Charleton said of this location: "That part of Riverside Newcastle ,.....smoke-blackened and neglected as it is.....presents a rare field to those who delight in the old-fashioned and the picturesque. To the casual visitor who crosses the Glasshouse Bridge the place, after the bustle and stir of the Quayside, appears to sleep a heavy and bedrugged sleep, disturbed now and then by the uneasy dreams of work; for whatever work goes on here is shut in by walls and palings, and gives no outer sign except it to be in the shape of additions to the already dense enough cloud of smoke which hangs overhead......."

The St. Peter's Works of R. & W.

Hawthorn would have certainly figured in this description. There was much transhipment of machinery from Hawthorn's Forth Banks Works (adjacent to Stephenson's Locomotive Works), which had become necessary owing to a slump in locomotive orders and an 1881 boom in marine engine orders. It was clear that Hawthorn required river frontage to progress, and soon this Works at St. Peters was working hand-in-glove with Charles Mitchell, supplying the majority of his ships with machinery.

In 1883, and in view of increasing technological complexity, the North East Coast Institution of Engineers and Shipbuilders was founded and the Chief Mechanical Engineer of

Above: Johnson tells us: "..Mr Ure commenced his attack on the formidable Bill Point and its opposite neighbours Bill Quay and Friar's Goose Points....without whose removal no improvements of the river would be complete...." Bill Point, up to the 1870s was a: " ..huge up-rearing cliff of 72 feet which protruded right into mid-stream" Only with its removal came the opportunities for Wood and Skinner to take advantage of a favourable flat-beach. By 1883 the yard also had the benefits of a well dredged water front and their shipbuilding business got under way. Until 1928, they constructed high quality iron ships of medium sizes, mainly cargo steamers and colliers; many lasted into the 1950s. Our view shows the traditional form of slipway building. Orders faded away after 1924, and by 1928, the majority of the workforce had drifted away and the concern closed. NMM, Greenwich/WSS.

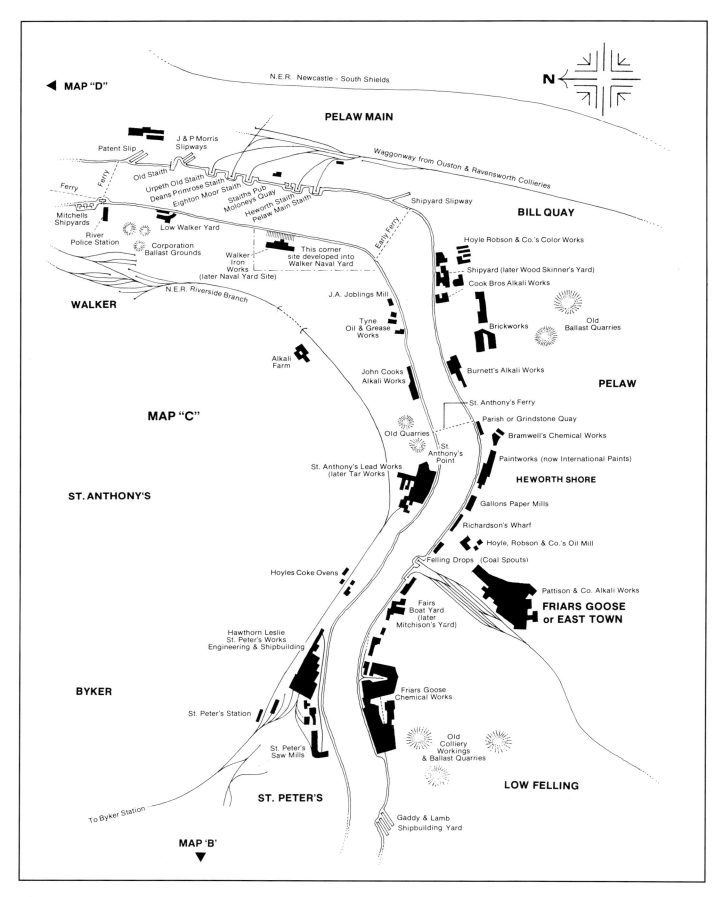

N

◀ MAP "D"

N.E.R. Newcastle - South Shields

PELAW MAIN

J & P Morris Slipways

Patent Slip

Ferry

Old Staith

Urpeth Old Staith

Deans Primrose Staith

Eighton Moor Staith

Staiths Pub Moloneys Quay

Heworth Staith

Pelaw Main Staith

Waggonway from Ouston & Ravensworth Collieries

Shipyard Slipway

BILL QUAY

Ferry

Mitchells Shipyards

River Police Station

Low Walker Yard

Corporation Ballast Grounds

Walker Iron Works (later Naval Yard Site)

This corner site developed into Walker Naval Yard

Early Ferry

Hoyle Robson & Co.'s Color Works

Shipyard (later Wood Skinner's Yard)

Cook Bros Alkali Works

Brickworks

Old Ballast Quarries

WALKER

N.E.R. Riverside Branch

J.A. Joblings Mill

Tyne Oil & Grease Works

Alkali Farm

John Cooks Alkali Works

Burnett's Alkali Works

PELAW

St. Anthony's Ferry

Parish or Grindstone Quay

Bramwell's Chemical Works

MAP "C"

Old Quarries

St. Anthony's Point

Paintworks (now International Paints)

St. Anthony's Lead Works (later Tar Works)

HEWORTH SHORE

ST. ANTHONY'S

Gallons Paper Mills

Richardson's Wharf

Hoyle, Robson & Co.'s Oil Mill

Felling Drops (Coal Spouts)

Hoyles Coke Ovens

Pattison & Co. Alkali Works

FRIARS GOOSE or EAST TOWN

BYKER

Fairs Boat Yard (later Mitchison's Yard)

Hawthorn Leslie St. Peter's Works Engineering & Shipbuilding

Friars Goose Chemical Works

St. Peter's Station

Old Colliery Workings & Ballast Quarries

St. Peter's Saw Mills

LOW FELLING

To Byker Station

ST. PETER'S

Gaddy & Lamb Shipbuilding Yard

MAP 'B' ▼

Above: The tug *Impetus* is here glimpsed wrestling with an unruly dockyard gate which appears to have shaken-off its tow-line en-route to it's new home. This April 1961 view clearly shows Hoyles Paintworks, nowadays (much extended) International Paints Ltd and a large riverfront landmark. To their right was once Wood Skinner's Yard 'stock' area. *South Shields Gazette.*

Hawthorn's, F. C. Marshall, played a large part in encouraging its growth. The following year, the two Hawthorn sites were managed separately. For many years, Marshall's excellent marine engines were second to none, as indicated by a well-filled order book; however, with the development of Parson's turbine, stiff competition was just around the corner.

The advent of the iron ship meant that bigger shipyards were needed and many small family shipyards, such as Gaddy & Lamb across the river, were to disappear, for after the 1860s building with iron became essential to survival.

We hear more about Andrew Leslie in the Map D area. Suffice to say here that an amalgamation of two companies with a fine maritime record brought about the formation of Hawthorn Leslie in 1886. The St. Peter's works continued to produce marine engines, whilst over the river, Fair's small beginnings had become the expanding shipyard of Mitchisons (1919). Tugs, trawlers and smaller craft came from this yard and in 1964, the Friars Goose Marina Management Group took over the slip.

Further along and past St. Anthony's Point eventually brings us to the site of Marconi Radar. At this site was the well-known Wood Skinner's yard. Operating by 1883, many fine steam 'tramps' and colliers were constructed, but fierce competition

had by 1924 driven orders elsewhere. Around the Bill Point, the still extant Harrison's slipway brings us into that stretch of river renowned the world over for its heavy shipbuilding industries. The north bank was covered with iron-works, graving docks, slips or huge stock-piling sheds. The south bank was, in contrast, the scene of frenzied coal teeming at the end of many North Durham pit railway links. The staiths had their own 'pub' amidst the coal-dust, known as Moloney's Bar after an interesting Irish character!

The shipyard owned by J.D. Morris, built next to an early defunct coal-spout, came and went within six years. As we approach Hebburn and the next map area, note the crossing place, until quite recently a Mid-Tyne Ferry landing. A photograph of one of their 'dumpy' vessels can be found on page **38**. It is shown adjacent to another of their principally workers-only floating landing-stages and gone by 1984.

Finally, we cast our eyes across for a final look along the north bank; note the remains of the 'Naval' yard opened in 1912 by Armstrong Whitworth to relieve their Elswick Yard. Many fine battleships including Queen Mary, Malaya, Nelson, Agincourt and King George V were built here, together with air-craft carriers. Closed in 1928, reopened and closed and again in 1931 and then again in

the mid-1970s, the yard had a somewhat chequered existence. The 1930s revival was solely due to Vickers transferring the building of the liner Monarch of Bermuda from the company's Barrow Yard. After the next naval boom during the Second World War, the yard settled down into building several passenger ships of high quality. In the mid-1950s, the yard constructed many high quality freighters for locally-managed shipping companies and eventually saw out its days fitting-out other yards products.

Charles Mitchell's yard, founded in 1853, was adjacent to the ferry. Even in 1867 this company's warships were armed by Armstrong though amalgamation didn't follow until 1882. Later to become Armstrong-Whitworth and eventually Vickers. In 1934, there were seven shipbuilding yards on the river containing 54 slips: the depression had closed 42 building slips within four years!

Right: A 1946 photograph illustrating the mass of shipping which was then a common sight in the middle reaches at Low Walker. Ships queued everywhere, awaiting attention after years of basic maintenance and excessive engine-hours. The standard wartime 'grey' pervades the scene, with one tug in unlined black and her name painted out. The large liner may have been the *Empire Deben* and according to local shipping enthusiast, George Scott, she was a post-war prize that had only recently been ceded to Britain. *University of Newcastle.*

Above: A wartime scene showing the cluttered Swan Hunter dry-dock with many vessels fitting-out at the riverside berths beyond. On the left is the Bowring Company's *Regent Panther*. Her two sisters: *Regent Lion* and *Regent Tiger* were both war losses. All three were in the 10,000 ton class and were built at Swan Hunter's yard upriver site during 1937-38. *Regent Panther* served her country until October 30 1959, when she arrived at Briton Ferry for breaking. *University of Newcastle.*

Above: The bend in the river that was, until 1880, almost impassible to larger ships due to the cliff outcrop at Bill Point. On the northern bank, at the extreme bottom is the location shown on Map C as the 'Tyne Oil & Grease Works, J.A. Jobling's Mill can be seen to have become an empty space before we reach the start of the Naval Yard at Low Walker. Around the bend to the north-east, the sheds once belonging to the Walker Iron Works of Losh, Wilson and Bell can be seen to have become 'absorbed' into the shipyard. The 'tidy' southern shore-line now belies the former chaotic 'staith-land' scenes. Only the small Harrison's slipway and the small craft around about show any signs of maritime activity here today. Nothing remains of the slipways of Wood Skinner's Yard at the bottom of the area in view. *University of Newcastle.*

Left: This fascinating and rare scene at Walker Naval Yard in the closing months of the last war ably illustrates the skills of the shipwright. These slips, at 1,100ft in length were the biggest on Tyneside at the time and could accommodate the longest required builds. The war years brought much work to the Tyne. *University of Newcastle.*

Section D

WALKER TO JARROW

A VERY large book would still be inaqequate to describe the enormous maritime progress credited to the yards of this section of river. We hardly need go two paces and we are upon the site of John Coutts yard, which is credited with the construction of the first large iron ship on the river, the Prince Albert, of 1842. This became the Neptune Yard, founded in 1860 by John Wigham Richardson, conveniently adjacent to Shaw's marine engine works. By 1903, this venture had joined forces with Swan Hunter, whose original yard was beyond the Hebburn/Wallsend ferry,

and in terms of industrial muscle were only eclipsed by the 140 acre Palmers' empire across the river. Strangely enough, Wallsend was originally best known throughout the world for its high quality coal. Johnson tells us: "in the late 1800s, Newcastle coal was ubiquitous, it was everywhere. European gas-works, Indian Mills, American railways, and coaling stations all over the world were fed with Newcastle coal. 'West Hartley' was as familiar a term to the foreign buyer as was 'Wallsend Main.'"

By the mid-19th century, coal

was receding from our riverfront scene and metal and chemical works prospered. The Tharsis Copper Works was on the site of the Willington Waggonway but this too disappeared to be replaced by the Willington (and later Clelands) shipyards....such was the pace of riverside evolution. We can't move far before viewing something of Swan Hunter's empire. This extended to a working area of 80 acres, and today huge oil rig modules are built in the yards of its former maritime neighbours at Howdon. One of these sites was the Wallsend Slipway Company

R.M.S. "MAURETANIA"

Facing page: At the turn of the century, Swan Hunter and Wigham Richardson amalgamated with the single aim of winning the biggest prize any yard in the world could hope for, at the time. This prestigious contract was for a Cunard Queen.....it was for RMS *Mauretania*. The rest, as they say, is history but the enormous pride felt in the North-East at winning the honour of building this ship still echoes through the years to the present day. Launched on September 20 1906 and completed by 1907, she had been constructed in her own special weatherproof shed; the fore-part was constructed first whilst plans were finalised for a revolutionary application of steam turbines. Even so, only 29 months elapsed from the contract being signed to delivery. She was undoubtedly quite special. Contempories say "..she was of unprecedented size and speed representing one of the greatest achievements of British Shipbuilding." Another account reported that the building was ".....the most stupendous task ever entrusted to a shipbuilder....for it involved the scientific solution of the most difficult problems in naval architecture and marine engineering...." (*Shipbuilder Magazine* Vol.1 Page 61) The *Mauretania* was 790ft long, 88ft wide and 60ft high. Accommodation was provided for 560 first, 500 second and no fewer than 1,400 third class passengers, whilst a crew of 800 brought capacity to a total of 3,260. Every passenger had 50% more accommodation space than any other top-class liner of the time. Her ornate decoration and luxurious appointments were incomparable with anything else and she quickly became known as 'the floating palace'. It seems she even had the edge of speed over her sister, the *Lusitania*, even though the latter did wrest the 'Blue Riband' title on two occasions. The *Mauretania* consistently dominated the Atlantic speed crossings, from her first run in 1907 until 1929. Unbelievably, in 1933, after having lost the Blue Riband to the *Bremen*, she very nearly won it back after running at 32 knots for 112 miles of the New York run – just two years away from retirement! Originally coal fired, she was converted to burn oil in 1921 and this further improved her performance. Faster competition, and old age finally took their toll and in the Autumn of 1934, after some short cruise work in all-over white livery, she was laid-up pending a decision over her future. It must have caused much heart-searching by the Directors of Cunard, but early in 1935 the decision was made to scrap her and on July 1 that year she sailed for Rosyth on her final voyage. Above right: A boat load of Newcastle dignitaries pay their last respects to Tyneside's pride off the mouth of the river of her birth, on July 3 1935. Messages were exchanged between her captain and the Mayor of Newcastle and later in the day she bade farewell forever to Tyneside, disappearing along the coast to the North for her last rendezvous. She had brought many bouquets to the Tyne and never once betrayed the skill and devotion invested in her by the builders. She will never be forgotten.
South Shields Library/John H. Proud; Courtesy of the family of W. Haig Parry.

where 'firsts' were a common occurence. They produced the first steel boiler on the Tyne in 1878 and had the honour of producing the steam turbines for the *Mauretania*. Closed in the mid-1980s, the site was cleared for oil rig construction. In between various Cement Works (which were also receding by 1900) was the North Eastern Marine Engineering Company, specialising in engines for its shipbuilding neighbours from 1882. NEM's 'bread and butter' product was its triple expansion steam machinery for 'tramps' and freighters large and small. Its huge electrically-operated crane of 1909 (with a lifting capacity of 150 tons) was – and remains - a landmark seen from as far as Morpeth. NEM became Clark-Hawthorn for a short time and today is known as Clark Kincaid.

To the north of Clelands, the 'Hadrian' yard was the site of the Tyne Iron Shipbuilding company, and lay adjacent to another branch of the Charles Palmer Empire. Maritime enthusiasts may remember the standard and highly successful 'C' design ships that became Tyne Iron's trade mark and more than 150 were built under franchise by other yards.

Few years could equal 1906 for maritime activity in this part of the Tyne. Nationally, things were changing. A new Liberal Government came to power and shipbuilding tonnage launched from the Tyne reached new heights. This year will be remem-

bered forever as the year the Tyne received the ultimate accolade...the order to build a major Cunard Liner...the *Mauretania*.

Wallsend owes much to George Hunter for this opportunity, for his energetic directorship paved the way towards the amalgamation with the Wigham Richardson company and the joint successful tender. Let's not forget the skill of Tynesiders. The building of this fast and beautiful ship was a great and glorious achievement to the men who worked on her. Besides the complications of providing power, she was very much a 'one-off', and thus challenged the workmen with considerable difficulties. Nevertheless, she always performed magnificently, reflecting Tyne shipbuilding at its finest. After many low points in shipbuilding, the 1940s and (unfortunately) the war-years, brought about changes that streamlined methods and put Swan Hunter in good shape for the 1950. In 1940, world shipping output was 1.7m tons – and Britain was responsible for almost half of this. Later, world output was 13.8m tons, but Britain was producing only 8%. This was not only the result of so much destruction in our ports and docks but a reflection on the 'conveyor-belt' style of ship production instituted by the USA. The Tyne still depended heavily upon traditional riveting techniques and during the war, the 54,000 shipyard workers in the North East

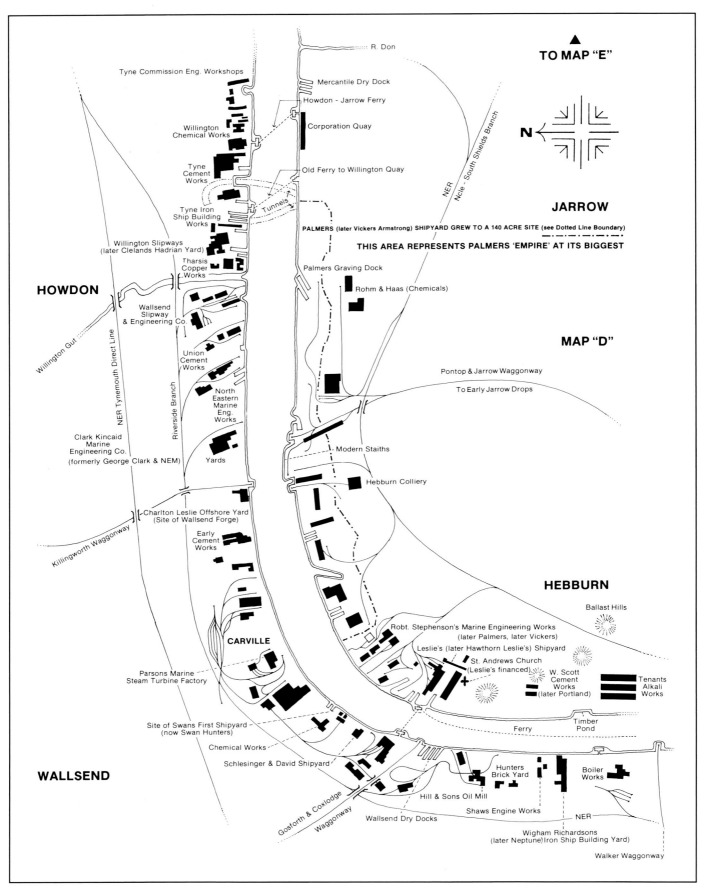

Tyne Commission Eng. Workshops

R. Don

Mercantile Dry Dock

Howdon - Jarrow Ferry

TO MAP "E"

N

Corporation Quay

Willington
Chemical Works

JARROW

Tyne Cement
Works

Old Ferry to Willington Quay

Tunnels

PALMERS (later Vickers Armstrong) SHIPYARD GREW TO A 140 ACRE SITE (see Dotted Line Boundary)

Tyne Iron
Ship Building
Works

THIS AREA REPRESENTS PALMERS 'EMPIRE' AT ITS BIGGEST

Willington Slipways
(later Clelands Hadrian Yard)

Palmers Graving Dock

Tharsis
Copper
Works

Rohm & Haas (Chemicals)

MAP "D"

HOWDON

Wallsend
Slipway
& Engineering Co.

Willington Gut

Pontop & Jarrow Waggonway

Union
Cement
Works

To Early Jarrow Drops

NER Tynemouth Direct Line

Riverside Branch

North
Eastern
Marine
Eng.
Works

Modern Staiths

Clark Kincaid
Marine
Engineering Co.
(formerly George Clark & NEM)

Yards

Hebburn Colliery

Charlton Leslie Offshore Yard
(Site of Wallsend Forge)

Early Cement
Works

HEBBURN

Killingworth Waggonway

Ballast Hills

CARVILLE

Robt. Stephenson's Marine Engineering Works
(later Palmers, later Vickers)

Parsons Marine
Steam Turbine Factory

Leslie's (later Hawthorn Leslie's) Shipyard

St. Andrews Church
(Leslie's financed)

W. Scott
Cement
Works
(later Portland)

Tenants
Alkali
Works

Site of Swans First Shipyard
(now Swan Hunters)

Chemical Works

Ferry

Timber
Pond

Schlesinger & David Shipyard

Hunters
Brick Yard

Boiler
Works

WALLSEND

Hill & Sons Oil Mill

Gosforth & Coxlodge
Waggonway

Wallsend Dry Docks

Shaws Engine Works

NER

Wigham Richardsons
(later Neptune) Iron Ship Building Yard)

Walker Waggonway

produced 500 merchantmen. Swan Hunter built an incredible 83 warships at their Tyne and Clyde yards.

Across the river now and at the east end of Hebburn Quay came a Shetland crofter called Andrew Leslie who was determined to build iron ships. A protege of Mitchell, Leslie formed a partnership with Coutts. The *Clarendon* was his first ship in 1854 and he showed dogged determination in the face of local Geordies who initially resented the Scots intrusion, but they soon came to love and respect him. 264 boats went down his slipways before amalgamation with R. & W. Hawthorn in 1886. By 1890, the yard was building cruisers such as HMS *Bellona* and in the 1920s ships for both P&O and Cunard were built. These orders helped the Company survive through a difficult spell and further built on their reputation, but by 1933 there was employment for only 650 men and just one vessel left the Hebburn slipway. The year 1937 brought fresh hope with the order for HMS *Manchester*, while 1938 saw the launch of HMS *Jervis* and HMS *Kelly*. Ship No. 615, flotilla leader *Kelly* was to capture the imagination of the nation under the command of Lord Louis Mountbatten when, in the words of the Naval Controller she "...was got into harbour not only by the good seamanship of the Officers and men,

but also on account of the excellent workmanship which ensured the water-tightness of the other compartments." *Kelly* had been towed from off the Norwegian coast after it was torpedoed on May 8 1940.

This yard's last ship the **Wiltshire,** of 10,036 tons in 1968, closed this particular chapter in a fine maritime tradition. Around St .Andrews Church, a Tyne landmark, some cranes remain and the yard offices are now a training centre for apprentices in shipbuilding. Ships may yet again be built at this historic location!

The next yard along belonged to Robert Stephenson and operated between 1886 and 1910, when slump prompted a takeover by the neighbouring Palmer yard. They left this site, only for it to be taken under the wing of another familiar name, Vickers-Armstrong. Shipbuilding recommenced in 1939, in time to fit-out the *Jervis Bay* for her armed merchantman's role. In the 1950s, almost £4 million was spent to bring the yard up to date, but vessels still outgrew facilities and closure

An anonymous wartime dry dock scene reveals damaged torpedo boats receiving attention. *South Shields Library.*

followed in 1970. More staiths are passed, before we come to perhaps the most incredible self-sufficient ship-making company on the river, Palmer's yard. Here, Charles Palmer established a considerable reputation for merchantmen. However, in the early 1900's, seven battleships were constructed here, including HMS *Lord Nelson*. She was virtually the last 'pre-Dreadnought' and was almost obsolete upon launch! This great shipyard started its decline in 1923, with closure of its steelworks, and the National Securities Company closed the main yard in 1933.

These yards will be remembered for the excellent working relationships between men and managers. Their closure rocked Hebburn and Jarrow as it accounted for 50% of local employment. The famous Jarrow march of 1936 was a consequence of this dire situation. The chemical company of Rohm and Hass now occupies part of the eastern end of the former Palmer site and keeps quite a few chemical tankers busy at its quay.

The old course of the River Don forms the limit to Map area D; its new course, around Jarrow Slake can be seen on Map E. This digest of interest in this area barely scraped the surface; anyone interested in further reading should check the bibliography on page 64.

Left: The first shipyard shown in Map D is the Neptune Yard, which eventually came under the control of Swan Hunter. Here, on January 20 1988, HMS *Chatham* was the last vessel to be launched from this famous slipway - the first having been in 1860! *Swan Hunter (SB) Ltd.*

Above: The arrival in the Tyne of the liner *Olympic* on October 13 1935 generated much interest at the riverside. She had been bought by Sir John Jarvis MP, to be broken at Jarrow and thus help relieve unemployment. When berthed alongside Palmers Yard, the sad process began immediately. Her sisters were the *Titanic* and the *Britannic*. The latter, completed in 1915, was taken over as a hospital ship and was sunk in the Aegean Sea on November 21 1916. Thus the *Olympic*, built in 1911 by Harland & Wolff Belfast, was the only one of the three sisters ever to trade commercially for the ill-fated White Star Line. Trading with the *Homeric* and the *Majestic* she did however help provide a balanced three-ship service on North Atlantic run at a time when a four-funnelled ship signified the last word in luxurious appointment. She made an unforgettable sight, even steaming to the breakers. *South Shields Library.*

Above: *Glenledi,* one of more than 50 Canadian 'Lakers' built by the SH&WR group of companies in the uncertain years of the mid-1920s for the grain and coal trade in the Great Lakes. She was built to fit the locks of the Welland Canal during her delivery voyage by the simple expedient of omitting 44ft of the midship hull! This was shipped out in pieces in the shortened ship's own hold and inserted in place by her owners following delivery. She saw service on the Lakes until scrapping in 1967. *Swan Hunter (SB) Ltd.*

Left: *Patris II*, moored at her birthplace of Swan Hunter & Wigham Richardson in 1926, was built for the Byron Steamship Company, to ply between the UK and the Mediterranean. She was subsequently sold to the Swedish Lloyd Company for the Gottenburg-London service; then, in 1935 she was chartered and subsequently sold to the Swedish Navy for conversion into a submarine depot ship. She was broken-up in 1971. *Swan Hunter (SB) Ltd.*

Left: *Meduana*, one of two French Liners built at Wallsend for Bordeaux-South American service and launched on September 30 1920. On November 22 that year, during fitting out, a fire was discovered on board which resulted in the loss of two lives. A great deal of loose shipyard equipment was on board and with the subsequent large amount of water pumped on board to quench the fire the ship keeled over. Raised in April 1921 she entered into service in November 1922. *Swan Hunter (SB) Ltd.*

Below: With *Mauretania*'s building shed in the background, the *Meduana* is seen after the fire and capsize, in company with the steam paddle tug *Enable.* Seized at Bordeaux by the Germans during the invasion of France, in the Second World War, she became a transport. Returned to French owners in 1947 and put to work on her original route, she was subsequently transferred to the Marseilles-Indo-China run. The ship was broken up in Antwerp in 1955. *Swan Hunter (SB) Ltd.*

Left: The *Mauretania's* building shed again dominates the background in this frenzied scene of Tyne activity in early 1944. Prominent in the picture is the tug *Wearmouth*, hauling the Swan Hunter floating crane *Titan II* up river. Fitting out on each side lie the Destroyers *Barfleur*, *Armada*, *Trafalgar*, *Sole Bay* and *St. Kitts*. These were 'Battle' Class destroyers, regarded by many as the most handsome ever seen upon the seas. Tyneside built half the entire class. They have now disappeared from our shores... many broken up on the north east coast. *University of Newcastle.*

Right: HMS *Illustrious*, launched in 1978, and seen that year at the fitting out quay near Walker Naval Yard . Her ski ramp take off deck looks curiously off balance from this low river viewpoint. She was at the time one of a new generation of mini-aircraft carriers long awaited by the Royal Navy to provide air cover for a task group of ships. A 'ski-ramp' fitted onto the bow of each ship gave the famous *Sea Harrier* a greater payload on take-off. Emergency accommodation was available to enable a full RM Commando detail to be carried and landed ashore. Dimensons: 206m x 32m x 6.5m. Displacement was 19,500 tons and speed 28 knots. Armament included four *Sea Dart* missile launchers and aircraft carried featured five *Sea Harriers* and 10 *Sea King* helicopters. HMS *Illustrious* was launched just too late to take part in the South Atlantic campaign of 1982. Her sister, HMS *Invincible*, launched from Vickers Barrow Yard in 1977, was quickly commissioned **and** of inestimable value in the Falklands conflict. She was the subject of a major re-fit in 1986. *Ken Groundwater.*

Left: Tyneside's earlier HMS *Superb*, launched in 1906, is seen off the mouth of the Tyne during trials in 1908. At this time the Government was in a fight for naval supremacy with Germany and of the three 'Dreadnoughts' ordered, Armstrong-Whitworth on the Tyne built one..... .against ferocious opposition! Many will remember the popular slogan at this time: 'We want eight (battleships) and we won't wait.' HMS *Superb* was the third in this series but the seventh RN ship to bear this proud fighting ship name. She was scrapped in 1922. *South Shields Library.*

Above: The Cruiser HMS *Superb* forms the centre piece of this mid-river view at Wallsend. She was built by Swan Hunter in the early 1940s and is seen here in 1956 during a refit prior to becoming a reserve fighting unit. In 1960 she was withdrawn and on August 8 1960 arrived at Troon for breaking. Her namesake and forerunner was also Tyne-built, in 1906 at Elswick. *South Shields Gazette.*

Above: Seen awaiting departure during sea trials in 1939 is HMS *King George V*. She is standing adjacent to her builders yard at Walker (Vickers-Armstrong) and took two years to build following the laying of her keel in January 1937. Her completion work accelerated considerably following the outbreak of war in September 1939 and, happily, she survived, making a tremendous contribution in the Far East. The days of big warships like this were numbered and she went to the breakers at Troon in 1959, only one year before the last battleship HMS *Vanguard*....thereby ending a chapter of naval history. *John H. Proud Collection*.

Right: Hawthorn Leslie's river frontage in May 1947, with the St. Andrew's Church a prominent feature. Leslie, the yard's maintenance ship is fussing about in front of HMS *Agincourt* and HMS *Alamein*, both 1943 'Battle' class destroyers. Also in the picture are the Shell tankers *Kelletia* and *Lampania*, with the *Auris* just visable on the stocks behind. *Laurence Dunn*

Left: The *Monarch of Bermuda* (see also the previous book in this SLP series, *Maritime Heritage, Barrow & Morecambe Bay*) built on the Tyne at Vickers Walker Yard, has returned from 'trooping' duties after the last war to undergo a much needed refit for its return to commercial operations. Behind, the P&O liner *Strathaird*, also receives a refit. *Laurence Dunn*.

Left: On the stocks at Hawthorn Leslie's Hebburn Yard in 1957 is the oil tanker *British Courage*. This view perhaps belies her 22,000 tons bulk, but it can be seen that dredging her launch channel is a priority. She was launched in that year and served until 1973 when she became the Pounentes under the Liberian flag. She eventually arrived at Kaoshing in 1978 for breaking, after suffering serious boiler damage on September 16 1976. This area now forms part of South Tyneside Council's Maritime Museum, where the cable ship *John W. Mackay* and HMS *Cavalier* lie, awaiting renovation. The cable ship was launched from the Neptune yard on November 30 1921. *John Johnson.*

Above and right: The age of the very-large oil tankers! This short (and for shipbuilders) expensive era dawned on the Tyne in 1970 and Swan Hunter made extensive replanning alterations within their empire to cope . The sky-high tonnage figures (*Esso Hibernia* was 126,539 tons gross) credited to Tyne output until 1977 had a sad aspect, however, in that many of these huge ships were subsequently laid-up following world recession biting deep and lessening oil demand. *Esso Hibernia* and *Tyne Pride* are two examples from the 1970-1976 period. Incredibly, some of the Esso tankers went for scrap within four years of launch, mainly due to what was then described as the uneconomic cost of maintaining steam-turbines in a mothballed condition. *Tyne Pride*, a speculative build by Swan Hunter, was more fortunate. After launch on October 6 1976, she was sold in November that year to the Tiger Shipping Company of Greece, and was renamed *Opportunity. University of Newcastle; John Johnson*

Above: The bend in the river between Wallsend and Hebburn, during the 1970s. On the left bank can be seen the floating landing stages of the Mid-Tyne ferry. Towering high at 'Swans' is a very large oil-tanker. It wiil be noticed that it is just about hanging over the Riverside branch railway line, which until circa 1980, was still bringing steel plate into dockland private sidings to the benefit of road users in the region. *University of Newcastle.*

Left: Blacksmiths at work in dry dock, repairing ships anchor cables....... their kind have long since gone. *South Shields Gazette.*

Left: The Willington Quay floating landing stage during a quiet spell on a lazy Sunday afternoon. Two trawlers are taking advantage of a cheap berth, lying adjacent to the *Tyne Princess*, the mid-Tyne ferry. The opening of the *Metro* rapid transit system prompted decline and closure for this ferry service during the 1980s, although in more recent times there have been proposals that it should be re-started. *South Shields Gazette.*

Below: An example of the work at Palmer's yard, during the company's heyday. A general cargo vessel, the Pear Branch was built in 1921 for Ritson of Sunderland. She is seen under tow by the paddle tug *Ulysses* of 1874 (bow) and *Francis Baty* (stern). This is an example of the work of local marine photographer Frank & Sons, of South Shields. His valuable negative collection was sadly destroyed and only a number of prints remain today as testimony to this fine collection. *South Shields Library.*

TYNE-BUILT SHIPS ALBUM

H.M.S. "NELSON"

Above: HMS *Nelson*, ordered to replace the earlier HMS *Lord Nelson* (see also page 1) left the Tyne in 1925 and survived to play a tremendously important role in the Mediterranean during the Second World War. She was eventually mined and torpedoed but neverthless survived to the end of hostilities. She was scrapped by Arnott Young's yard at Troon, in Ayrshire, in the early 1950s. *South Shields Library.*

Right: HMS *Queen Mary* was another example of a Tyne early post-Dreadnought ship which subsequently took part on May 31 1916 in the Battle of Jutland in the First World War. As one of Admiral Beatty's Battlecruisers, she made the initial engagement with the German Battlecruisers. However, The Royal Navy quickly learned that speed and fire-power were for nought if accurate fire-control and armour weren't comprehensive. Very early in the engagement, she was under an intense pounding from both *Seydlitz* and *Derfflinger*. With frightening suddeness, a shell penetrated her magazines and the ship exploded; within minutes she sank with terrible loss of life. *South Shields Library.*

Left: *Turbinia*. Little needs to be said that isn't already known in connection with this tiny vessel, which rocked the maritime world at the Spithead naval review of 1897. In an era of reciprocating steam engines, her turbines revolutionised propulsionand not just in the context of shipping, but also eventually for aircraft and power stations the world over. The orders for turbines rolled in and the name of Charles Parsons was to be known throughout the world in a very short time. Built at Wallsend, the vessel is preserved as a proud part of Tyne history. *South Shields Library.*

Below: HMS *Terror*. The Tyne led the early way in building heavy armour-plated battleships when, in 1856, Sir Charles Palmer built *Terror* at his already well-known yard. This ship proved the superiority of rolled iron plating for armour clad ships, and in so doing, Palmer emerged as the leading naval shipbuilder outside the naval dockyards. HMS *Terror* eventually became a depot ship at Bermuda, until 1901. She was the seventh of 10 ships to carry this fighting name. *South Shields Library.*

Below left: *Gripsholm*, of 1925, was a fine compact liner and capable of 30 knots, a respectable speed. Built by Armstrong-Whitworth for the Swedish-America Shipping Line, she was ultimately bought by North German Lloyd in the 1950s and sailed as the Berlin until 1966, when she finally went to Italian breakers after an illustrious career of 41 years. *WSS.*

Below right: A 1922 build by Armstrong-Whitworth, *Ausonia* was one of four Tyne-built sisters for Cunard, ordered to replace First World War losses. Requisitioned by the Admiralty and converted as an armed cruiser in 1939, she was eventually purchased by the British Government in 1944 to take on the new role of a heavy repair ship. Returning to 'line' duties after refurbishment, she was eventually sold to Spanish breakers in 1965, a credit to her builder. *Laurence Dunn.*

Left: *Dominion Monarch*. No sooner had this vessel been launched from Swan Hunter's slipways than she was requisitioned as a troopship for use in the last war. Her career was almost cut very short when she was in Singapore at the precise time that the Japanese troops invaded. Fortunately, she raised steam quickly and escaped the harbour in the 'nick of time!' She eventually got around to her true vocation by December 1948, and after refurbishment, entered into service on the London-Australia/New Zealand run. Ironically, she was sold to the Japanese in 1962 (who simply added 'MARU' to the end of her name) She was converted as a floating hotel and the ship was used in a final blaze of glory at the Seattle World Fair. Then, her purpose complete, she was sold to breakers in Osaka. She was a handsome ship, seen here in the River Thames, outward bound in July 1958. *Laurence Dunn.*

Left: *Ocean Monarch*. was built by Vickers Yard in 1951. She was a cruise-only ship for Furness Withy, but designed to please a new emerging American middle class. Eventually, cheap flights competing on her route to Bermuda placed her future in doubt by the mid-1960s. By September 1966 she was laid-up in a creek in the River Fal, awaiting a buyer. She was eventually sold in 1967, resold in 1978 and finally gutted by fire in Greece as the *Riviera*. This was a sad end to a very handsome ship. *Laurence Dunn.*

Right: *Empress of England* was launched at Vickers' Walker Yard on May 8 1956 and left the river of her birth on the March 16 1957. Her maiden voyage from Liverpool was on April 18 1957, when this picture was taken as she prepared to serve for Canadian Pacific, (Elder Dempster's *Apapa* is astern) The ship had a serious collision in the St. Lawrence River in November 1965, when her passengers were evacuated. In 1970, she was sold to Shaw Savill for £5 million who renamed her *Ocean Monarch*, a name carried by the earlier Tyne liner pictured above. Her new name didn't bring good fortune and after many problems (including crewing difficulties) she left Southampton on June 13 1975 for Taiwan breakers. *Laurence Dunn.*

Below: *City of Lahore* was built at Palmer's at Hebburn in 1911. A sister ship followed shortly after from the same yard and was named *City of Birmingham*. *City of Lahore* is seen sporting Bucknall's distinctive diamond logo on her funnel in October 1931 in Cape Town Bay....a far cry from the perhaps less colourful banks of the Tyne! The ship was scrapped in 1933. *Laurence Dunn*

Right: One of six post-war Cunarders ordered with Tyne builders, *Ascania* was launched from Armstrong-Whitworth's Yard in 1925 for the London-Canada service. In December 1934 she rescued the crew of locally manned SS *Usworth*, in trouble in mid-Atlantic. She was requisitioned as an armed merchant cruiser during the Second World War and went trooping'until 1943. She was then converted as an infantry landing ship, reverting to her former role as a troopship in 1944 until the end of hostilities. After modifications, with a much needed refit in 1949, she was fit to resume her commercial duties and was broken up at Newport, South Wales in 1957, after a very useful career. *Laurence Dunn.*

Right: In comparison with the *Dominion Monarch* (see page 41) it can be seen that the *Perseus* (Vickers, 1950) was to be a 'working' ship! The decline in patronage by passengers as air travel became more commonplace forced owners to veer towards greater versatility and the *Perseus* met these objectives admirably. She first came to the media's attention when, in June 1965, she collided with the *Kinross* in the Suez Canal. Again in the news in August 1970, she rescued 40 crew and two passengers from the *Don Jose Figueras*, which was on fire in the Pacific. She ended her days in 1973 on a beach in Taiwan. *Laurence Dunn.*

Left: Built in 1925 by Hawthorn Leslie, *Ranchi* was another ship commandeered from P&O for use as an armed merchant cruiser in 1939. It survived the war and was refitted in in 1948 to return to service as a single-funnelled liner. Gross tonnage was 16, 738 and she was scrapped in 1953. She is seen here at Port Said in 1934. *Laurence Dunn.*

Right: In 1922-23, Hawthorn Leslie provided the British India Line with two sister-ships. The first was *Talma* (shown here), the other the *Tilawa*. Capable of carrying more than 1,000 passengers in her three classes, she was a success in her far eastern trading. The *Tilawa* unfortunately did not survive the Second World War, being torpedoed by the Japanese in 1942. *Talma* was broken up at Inverkeithing in 1949, after giving her river of birth three long blasts whilst passing en route North on her final voyage. Our picture shows her on trial in September 1923. *Laurence Dunn.*

Right: *Antenor*, was built by Palmers in 1925 for the China Mutual Shipping (Blue Funnel Line). Her sisters were *Hector*, *Sarpedon* and *Patroclus*. All except the last were Tyne-built. *Antenor* returned to the North-East infrequently, but she made her last voyage to the area of her birth, to Blyth, for scrapping in 1953. *WSS.*

Above: Bringing us up to date is the penultimate liner built on the Tyne and bestowed upon her was a fitting name....*Northern Star*. She was very much a 'new look' to river craftsmen with her funnel 'aft' and many other details breaking a few 'traditional' rules. Launched from Vickers Armstrongs by Her Royal Highness Queen Elizabeth the Queen Mother she went into service for Shaw Savill & Albion, leaving the river in 1962. After a few initial 'teething' troubles she settled down to a period of solid service, but as the 1960s passed the writing was very much 'on the wall' for her type as the custom for which she had been built had all but gone by 1970. She thus went prematurely to the ship-breakers in December 1975. *Roger Woodcock Collection.*

HOWDON TO PERCY MAIN

Above: This is a rare view (circa 1919/20) of a timber-built floating dock, adjacent to Tyne Dock Engineering Works. It shows the Ridley steam tug *Oscar* being reboilered. When she came from her previous port, Dundalk, she had two funnels. *South Shields Library*.

THE Tyne Improvement Commission certainly made early improvements in this area and within seven years of its inauguration in 1928 invited the Duke of Northumberland to an area which had once been open fields (below an obscure colliery village called Percy Main) to open Northumberland Docks. Soon, 50% of the output from the Blyth and Tyne area pits was making for the dock and, as seen by the map, they may have shared 'metals' but they nevertheless divided towards their respective colliery staiths for teeming to 'dedicated' trading partners. Their coal was best quality steam-coal or bunker-coal, and the docks soon became popular for 'topping-up' the bunkers of passing ships.

Prior to this, the pits only other outlet had been via small private harbours at Seaton Sluice and Blyth.

At Blyth, the water depth was such that only ships of small size could load. Consequently, foreign trade suffered badly, until the advent of **Northumberland** Dock. This brings us to a most incredible maritime story as reported in the *Newcastle Daily Chronicle* on December 4 1901......but referring to 1842!

The report said: "The Bedlington Coal Company had just adopted a novel method of shipping their coals in the Tyne. Loaded chaldron waggons, 40 at a time, were conveyed by an iron twin-screw steamer Bedlington, especially contructed for the purpose, from the staiths on the north side of the river Blyth......to Shields Harbour on the Tyne. They were there discharged into colliers by means of steam derricks with which the vessel is provided." The difficulties of competing with collieries

having direct Tyne access can easily be seen to have driven Northumbrians to unreasonable lengths, but one has to applaud their determination. It was another four years before the Northumberland Dock and Percy Main Branch Railway Act was passed under the guidance of that railway scoundrel, George Hudson. Incidentally, the Bedlington, built at Marshall's (South Shields) was sold in April1851 and was bought for service as a ferry on the Forth.

The Tyne Commissioners became involved with railway operations and it will be seen on this map that they had their own Commissioners railway

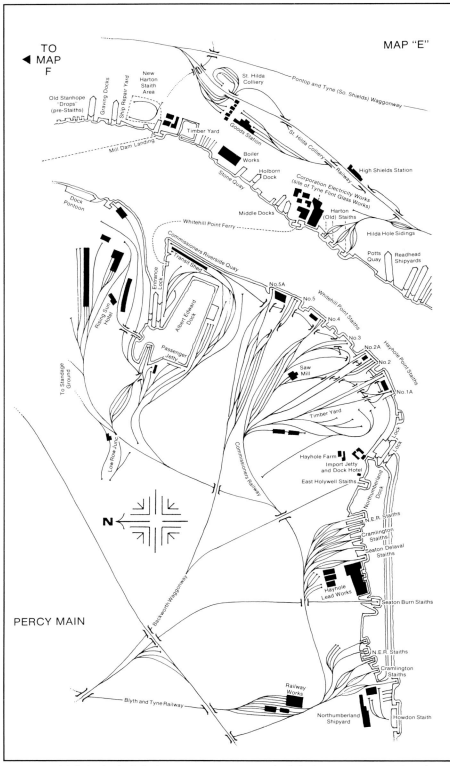

New Harton Staith Area

St. Hilda Colliery

Pontop and Tyne (So. Shields) Waggonway

Old Stanhope "Drops" (pre-Staiths)

Graving Docks

Ship Repair Yard

Timber Yard

Goods Station

St. Hilda Colliery Railway

High Shields Station

Mill Dam Landing

Boiler Works

Stone Quay

Holborn Dock

Corporation Electricity Works (site of Tyne Flint Glass Works)

Dock Pontoon

Middle Docks

Harton (Old) Staiths

Hilda Hole Sidings

Whitehill Point Ferry

Commissioners Riverside Quay

Transit Shed

Entrance Lock

Potts Quay

Readhead Shipyards

Rising Sun Hotel

Albert Edward Dock

No.5A

No.5

Whitehill Point Staiths

No.4

No.3

Hayhole Point Staiths

Passenger Jetty

No.2A

No.2

To Standage Ground

Saw Mill

No.1A

Timber Yard

Low Row Junc.

LOCK

Commissioners Railway

Hayhole Farm

Import Jetty and Dock Hotel

East Holywell Staiths

Northumberland Dock

N

N.E.R. Staiths

Cramlington Staiths

Seaton Delaval Staiths

PERCY MAIN

Hayhole Lead Works

Seaton Burn Staiths

Backworth Waggonway

N.E.R. Staiths

Cramlington Staiths

Railway Works

Blyth and Tyne Railway

Northumberland Shipyard

Howdon Staith

system, which included their own signalboxes, staff and engines, a couple of which will be noted in these pages. They maintained the tracks to Hayhole.Point and Whitehill Point Staiths and, eventually, with the advent of the docks at Albert Edward,

extended their system in 1928 to their own Tyne Commissioners Quay and a passenger service connection with North Sea ferries. This service still operates today, but the surroundings are perhaps the least inspiring of the current maritime scene along the

Tyne. The Northumberland Docks are now completely filled, up to the breakwater line on the map. The Hayhole Lead Works remains as an inhospitable island amidst wasteland and seemingly abandoned lorry trailers. It seems that opportunities to attract a direct rail/sea container ro/ro link have been missed and the price is paid with constant threats of closure to the ferry service. The Albert Edward Dock survives and still attracts shipping, and the remains of the double-sided staith can still be seen in 1990.

Whitehill Point last saw coal shipments in 1974 and the site is now lost under parked containers. Adjacent to the old lock gates is the Tyne Tanker Cleaning Company, helping reduce pollution in the environment.

We now turn our attention to that area of High Shields across the river where, thanks to historian Amy Flagg, we know a lot more about the beginnings and methods of early shipbuilding. Many thought that the docks adjacent to Potts Quay was the beginning of it all but Amy tells us: "..legend (says) that the first dock in the town was built by the Wallis family on the site occupied....by John Readhead & Son, and known as the West Docks. The dock constructed by John,Thomas and William Wallis was the High Dock at the junction of Commercial Road and West Holborn, and occupied for many years by the related firms of Straker, Edwards and Smith; and, in any case, it was not the first dock in the town, this honour (fell) to the Low Dock in Wapping Street."

These West Docks are shown as 'Readhead Shipyard' on our map and, she adds later, were planned, laid out and occupied on agricultural land by a Sunderland firm in 1811. Potts Quay, nearby, was eventually built into for a dock and in 1822 was "... sold by Mr.James Young to Messrs Readhead & Co; iron shipbuilders..." So began a story that lasts to this day,and their first ship, the Jane Kilsall was launched in January 1882. Now, along a little to Middle Docks and No.1 dock here is the original facility of about 1768, (although much enlarged). The first Middle Dock Company built small wooden ships up to 1899 when it became the

Middle Dock and Engineering Company. They built the No. 3 Dock to 460ft and extended into the Holborn Dock following the departure of Eltringham & Co. In more modern times, Readhead's are remembered for their long associations with the shipping lines of Haines, Runciman's and Strick. In 1968, they became another 'arm' of Swan Hunter, but in 1970 shipbuilding became ship repairing only.

The Stone Quay, originally built for shipping limestone from the quarries at Cleadon, was the centre of a group of salt-pans in mid-18th century. About 1878, Mr J.T. Eltringham acquired the site and forever after it became associated with his boatyard. The company had begun at the Middle-Landing area and was very well known at the turn of the century for its fine paddle steamers, tugs and, later, steam trawlers. By 1907 the yard had built 26 trawlers for the Prince Fishing Company, of North Shields, but one of the best known ships was the tug *Great Emperor*. She was built for John Dry Steam Tugs in 1909 and eventually passed to Messrs France Fenwick of Newcastle. The *Shields Gazette* reported, on Febuary 5 1959: "This week has seen the passing of one of the Tyne's oldest steam tugs, the *Great Emperor*. She is now at King's Yard at Gateshead, for breaking up. When she was built fifty years ago at the old Eltringham Yard she was regarded as the pride of the Tyne tugs and looked upon as such for as many years; but (she) has been lying idle and out of service for the past 8 weeks and now she comes under the breakers' hammers...."

MAP E 1

THE STANHOPE & TYNE RAILWAY first built coal drops (as shown on Map E on the very top left-hand side) just east of the Harton 'new' staiths of today. Their modest facilities were clearly ill-conceived and, together with copious land purchased along the Stone Quay area by the Brandling Railway Company were all aborted when the Stanhope & Tyne Railway went bankrupt and their own plans for a massive coal shipping dock was similarly aborted. A Tyne Dock Company was formed on July 1 1839 by Act of Parliament, and this scheme was eventually developed by the NER. Excavations for the dock were suspended in 1849 and a new Act was obtained in 1854 including even more enlarged facilities. In January 1859, coal finally started to pass through the dock, and, as will be seen from our map, it was constructed on the eastern fringe of that area known as Jarrow Slake........even today, a bleak muddy estuary.

Designed for the NER by local engineer Mr. T Harrison, it was declared the largest coal dock in the world and certainly remained so until the late 19th century. Its main basin consisted of a 50 acre area and four main jetties, accompanied by numerous smaller 'spouts' and cargo handling berths. At the time of planning, it was (bearing in mind the average size of the sailing vessels then predominant in the coal trade) intended to accommodate up to 500 vessels.

When the coal began to flow, it meant that all the slow one-wagon spouts became extinct and the colliers no longer had to wait for a week at a time at the buoys in the coal queue. The Tyne coal-rush had begun, and as fast as shipbuilders produced colliers, Londoners begged for even more. The coal-owners continually raised the keel-rates and the shipping agents/owners similarly profited from the trade. The overall Tyne shipment figure in 1859 was four million tons, this jumped to more than ten million tons by 1890 and reached a peak in exces of 21 million tons in 1923, before industrial strife laid low river produce.

By 1934, Tyne Dock had shipped an incredible 323 million tons of coal; an astounding figure. The rails to the staiths passed over a busy road at their 'neck' and this noisy black tunnel was known to generations as the 'arches'. Beyond were 25 miles of sidings all of which passed over to the Port of Tyne Authority in the 1940s. Our photographs depict the Dock from 1922 to 1965, when infilling got under way.

Above: This relatively up-to-date view in 1976, looks down on the entrance of both Albert Edward and Tyne Docks. When compared to our map showing the 1900 situation a great difference immediately strikes the observer. Very evident is how the once numerous railway network has retreated, likewise a deal of industry, which has sadly left huge tracts of barren and often contaminated land. To the bottom of the view adjacent to the oil storage tanks is the now filled entrance to Northumberland Dock. A new road comes right through the heart of the old coal shipping dock. It is heartening to see at least a limited amount of shipping along the southern Shields shore. A ship is moored to the remains of the staith at Hayhole Point and a North Sea ferry is at Tyne Commissioners Quay, with some boats inside Albert Edward Dock. *University of Newcastle.*

Above: The 1950 saw some visits to the Tyne by the *Dunera*. Built by Barclay Curle in 1937 (12,615 gross tonnage). Her first owners were British India lines but she was completed as a troopship. She later became a school ship and is seen on an educational venture. She ended her days at **Bilbao** in November 1967. The tugs are the *Beamish* (left) and *Maximus*. *John Johnson.*

Right: A modern day Ro/Ro car ferry at the Commissioners Quay. This 1980 scene shows the Norwegian *Venus*, not seen so often today. The *Venus* is otherwise known as the *Black Prince* in her Winter role, when cruising to Madeira. As I write, in 1990, the car ferry *Auto Route* is off-loading 600 new Volvo cars at Albert Edward Dock, but little else on this scale now occurs at these once busy docks. *Ken Groundwater.*

Above: An evocative view of coaling at Howden Staiths in 1959. One of the Hudson boats of the John Hudson Fuel & Shipping Company, *Hudson Strait* was completed in 1946 by the Ailsa SB Company, Troon at 2,904 gross tons. She became *Camelina* in 1967. The 1940s craftmans work on the proud wooden bridge is plain to see. *John Johnson.*

Below: A 1959 scene at the upper bend in the river, as shown in Map E. The launch of the *Granwood* (7,919 GRT) from John Readheads High Shields Yard, whilst the tug *George V* prepares to take charge of the hull. The *Bristol City* stands at the fitting-out berth. Granwood was sold to Ofmike Corporation in 1971 and became the *Penny Michaels. John Johnson*

Above: It's June 9 1954 at Mill Dam landing as a couple of gentlemen observe the *Beeding* being manoevred for Harton Staiths. Adjacent, a Tyne Improvement Commission dredger is deepening the 'ways'. The *Beeding*, (1,142 GRT), built at Goole for Stephenson Clarke Shipping in 1950, was taken over by Kelly's of Belfast in 1970 to become the *Ballymore*. By 1975 after a further sale she was seen as the *Baltica*. Her sad end came in 1977 when, after striking an underwater object between Spezia and Barcelona, she was abandoned by her crew to become beached; she was later broken up where she lay. *South Shields Gazette.*

Below: In 1959, the Swan Hunter ship *Leda* (6,670 GRT) stands at Commissioners Quay whilst passengers embark. Passing is the collier *Ardingly*; over towards South Shields is *Dunera* leaving the river for a cruise. *John Johnson.*

Above: A detail view of loading operations on the Commissioners Quay as the *Leda* receives its cargo, in 1959. Carrying cars aboard ship involved delicate operations like this in the days before roll-on-roll-off ships appeared. *John Johnson.*

Above: An unusual view of an unusual vessel. Built on the Tees in 1941 as a landing craft, 'BPV2' came to the Tyne during 1942 for re-arming at Palmers, Jarrow. She is seen after the conversion, off the Northumberland dock 'boom' in 1942, complete with her banks of armament: eight 2pdr 'pompoms' (staggered port and starboard) and 4 Oerlikons, complete with full crew. She was sunk in action in 1944, one of only six BPV bombardment vessels. Note the Hayhole Lead Works in the background. *John H. Proud/Courtesy the family of W. Haig Parry.*

Above: This fine five-mast collier barque is seen at the staiths within Albert Edward Dock in 1901. She was constructed at Henderson's yard at Partick, on the Clyde, in 1890. At 6,200 DWT and at 361ft in length she was one of the larger boats built for French shipping agents A.D. Bordes. Few will deny her beauty. Her clean steel plating and fine sheer would have made her a fine sight running down the 'easters.' Alas, this picture is believed to be the last one taken of her, for she was abandoned and lost in May 1901 with a cargo of Tyne coals (seen here being loaded) for Valparaiso. *John H. Proud/Courtesy the family of W. Haig Parry.*

Above: This 1958 Albert Edward Dock view underlines the importance of timber to the economics of northern ports. From Hartlepool to Blyth, the coal industry demanded many a thousand tons of pit props and A.B. Bore of Slottesgatam, Finland, was a regular supplier. His varied fleet displayed the family name, plus a number and this is *Bore IX* , after arrival with a cargo of props. She was built by MacMillan, on the Clyde, for Burrell & Sons of Glasgow, eventually coming into the hands of the Bore group in 1921. Her 'cruiser-stern' speaks of another age. Sadly, she arrived in Hong Kong for breaking on the May 27 1959, not long after this 1958 picture was taken. This was one of her last payloads and perhaps her final trip to the North East. *John Johnson.*

Below: This view within Tyne Dock shows the Tyne built *Obra* loading cargo for the far-east, in 1946. She had been completed that year by Readhead's, for British India Steam Navigation, and it is safe to assume that this is probably her maiden voyage, bearing in mind her condition for 1946! *University of Newcastle.*

Below: Cars - even in 1990 – play a big part in the commercial viability of Edward Albert Dock, although today they are imported rather than exported. This nostalgic 1959 scene sees a boatload of Austin *Westminster* saloons awaiting export. The Spanish-built *El Salazar*, owned by Nav Del Atlanticos, is embarking a cargo of salt. *John Johnson.*

Above: A view around the North-west Quay area within Tyne Dock. The 200-acres Dock Estate was taken over by the Tyne Improvement Commission, from the LNER, in the 1940s. This view illustrates a common discharging method for timber cargoes and although few can claim to 'walk-on-water'....these men seem to have mastered the skill! The men 'in' the dock, would tether the wood to prepare for a launch dragging it to wet storage elsewhere. Blue Star line's *Tacoma Star* would perhaps find the surroundings a little drab in comparison with the many exotic locations she would have visited overseas. She had disappeared from the scene by 1973. *John Johnson.*

Above: The ore 'grabs' are hard at work in this September 1961 view showing Tyne Dock's riverside berth adjacent to Sutherland Dock. The ore, from Sweden, will soon be transported by the hilly railway to Consett, to serve the insatiable appetite of the steelworks, of which no trace remains today. The *Torne*, built in 1959, as an ore carrier for the Swedish Company of Grangesberg-Oxelosund, became the Tornado in 1970, after conversion as an oil carrier sailing under the Finnish flag. *South Shields Gazette.*

Right: A frozen scene in Tyne Dock during 1982. The Port of Tyne Authority considered hiring ice-breakers for the first time ever during this January cold spell. *South Shields Gazette.*

Above: This immensely interesting photograph of Tyne Dock in circa 1922 is a flashback to the days when the North-East ports were a constant forest of masts and funnels. This was at the peak of business on the river - never would river 'Geordies' see these massed sights again. Providing a permanent record of this great age is such a picture as this, Prominent is the *Schieland*. She was built by Smulders (Holland) in 1916 for a coal shipping company. A survivor of the First World War, she became a victim of the Second, being sunk in 1941. Built on the Tyne at North Shields by T .& W. Smith as the *Dunstanborough* back in 1871, she was given her new name by 1922 owner Gustav Salling, her port of registry being Flensburg, Germany. *South Shields Gazette.*

Right: An interesting aerial view of Tyne Dock, circa 1964, with only staith number four in situ and operating. At this time, the finale of the Dock's 120 year maritime coal export business was approaching. The complex layout of railway sidings and the staiths they supplied is clearly shown. *University of Newcastle.*

Above: We cannot leave Tyne Dock without first reviewing the shipping in this packed 1950 scene at Tyne Dock. First, the *Broadhurst*: she was built in 1948 by Grangemouth Dockyard for our local shipping agents Stephenson, Clarke. The ship ended her days at Blyth breakers October 1968. Behind her is the *Avisbrook*, built in 1943 at the famous Hartlepool Yard of William Gray as the *Empire Harmony*, she was the carrying the name *Capetan Panaos* when she made her last journey to the breakers at Piraeus, in 1969. Adjacent is *Wanda*, dating back to 1897. She was built abroad as the *Skanderborg*, receiving her later name in 1933 and retaining it until 1955 when she became the *Ridal*. She went for scrap in October 1958, at 61 years of age. In the centre background is the *Gudrun*, (with a 'T' on the funnel). Built at Kiel in 1924 for Torm's of Copenhagen, she was renamed *Gudrun Torm* in 1951 and the reason is interesting. The Danish Government was tired of the confusion being caused by many Danish ships carrying the same female name. They thus decreed that, where a ship had a girl's Christian name, it must have a second name to qualify it. Hence *Gudrun* took onboard her owners name ...Torm! *South Shields Gazette.*

Section F

NORTH AND SOUTH SHIELDS

THE early growth of salt-making at South Shields is presumed to be connected with easily exploited coal measures. There are references to salt pans in 1499, but it was in the 17th century that we learn how intense the business was, when a contempory travellor reported "...at Sheeldes...I viewed the salt-works wherein is more salt-works and more salt made than in any part of England I know........" A century later, in 1750, a map-maker commented: "....South Shields, the station of the sea coal fleets, is a large village eminent for its saltworks – here being upwards of 200 pans for boiling the sea water into salt..." Even so, shipbuilding was making its presence felt and in Amy Flagg's book, we are told: "...the eastern extremity of the old township of South Shields was the birthplace

and for long the nursery of shipbuilding in our town....."

She may as well have been refering to the area up to say St Peters, for shipbuilding arrived here early in time, and the slipways that Amy refers to, are shown on our map in their approximate location, bearing in mind the inaccuracy of early maps. She managed to trace the history of this area from 1729 through to 1919 and says that its history "is practically serial." There were many shipbuilders which had a relatively short life in the trade, such were its fluctuations, here is a summary of some examples: William and Catherine Forster c1773-1791; James Evans & Son 1788-1831; John Wright 1773-1803; Attley, Swan & Brown 1803-1808; J. & P. Laing 1818-1830 (Eventually of Wearside fame!) and Thomas W. Wawn 1846-

1852. Some were longer lasting: J.P. Rennoldson & Son 1863-1929; John Readhead & Co. 1872-1968; Hepple & Co. 1899-1924; Thomas Forsyth & Co. 1806-1858 and H.S. Smith Edwards, 1856-1899. This last company became the Middle Dock Engineering Company; bringing us to the oddest story of all .....Simon Temple & Son, 1780-1810.

Simon Temple had a yard 'somewhere in Holborn ' with another at the eastern docks, or a predecessor of the Tyne Dock Engineering Company. The first mention of the firm's naval connection comes in 1799. On almost every ship he failed to meet the agreed delivery date for the Admiralty, and it can only be assumed that he was heavily penalised. In spite of this, Temple's Son continued to receive naval patronage. It was in

Above: A tantalising glimpse into the past in a broad river sweep from Smiths Dock (on the left) to Brigham's Dry Dock (right). Prominent is the Gas Light & Coke steam collier *Fireside*, awaiting a berth at Harton Staiths. She was built at S.P. Austin's Yard for the power company and served London's firesides until

1962 when she was bought by a Panamanian concern to become *Dynamikos*. In 1965, she became *Nikos V* but was wrecked two miles off Driana Lighthouse in December 1967. Note the TIC Dredger discharging silt into a TIC steam hopper.
South Shields Gazette.

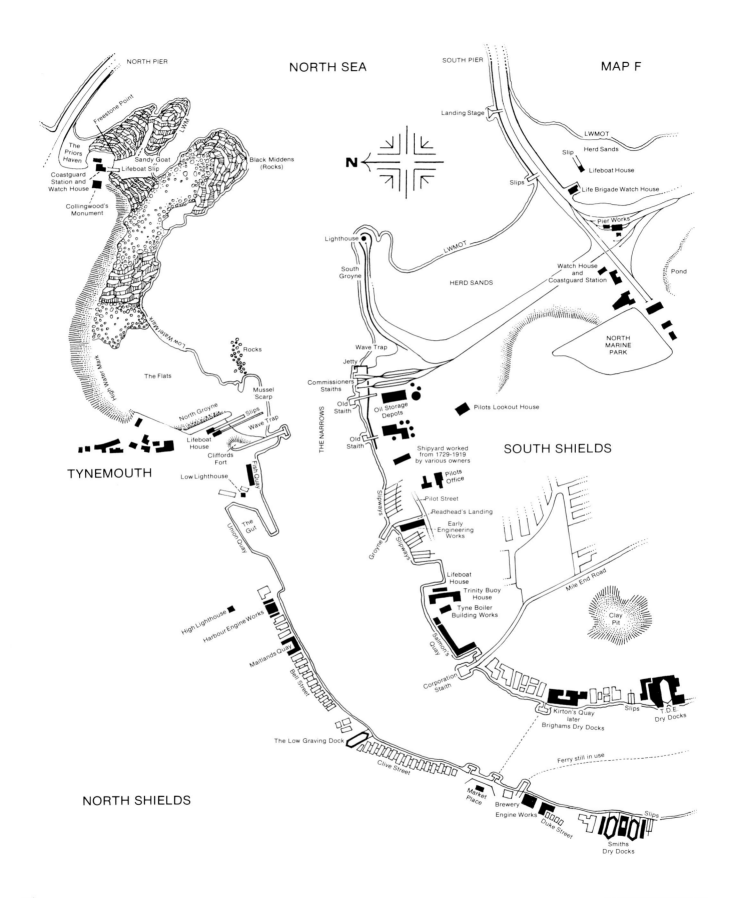

NORTH PIER

NORTH SEA

SOUTH PIER

MAP F

Freestone Point

LWM

Sandy Goat

The Priors Haven

Lifeboat Slip

Black Middens (Rocks)

Coastguard Station and Watch House

Collingwood's Monument

N

Landing Stage

LWMOT

Slip

Herd Sands

Lifeboat House

Life Brigade Watch House

Slips

Pier Works

Lighthouse

South Groyne

LWMOT

HERD SANDS

Watch House and Coastguard Station

Pond

NORTH MARINE PARK

Rocks

The Flats

High Water Mark

Low Water Mark

Mussel Scarp

North Groyne

Slips

Wave Trap

Lifeboat House

Cliffords Fort

Low Lighthouse

Fish Quay

The Gut

Union Quay

TYNEMOUTH

Wave Trap

Jetty

Commissioners Staiths

Old Staith

THE NARROWS

Old Staith

Oil Storage Depots

Shipyard worked from 1729-1919 by various owners

Pilots Lookout House

SOUTH SHIELDS

Pilots Office

Groyne

Slipways

Slipways

Pilot Street

Readhead's Landing

Early Engineering Works

Lifeboat House

Trinity Buoy House

Tyne Boiler Building Works

Mile End Road

Clay Pit

High Lighthouse

Harbour Engine Works

Maitlands Quay

Bell Street

Salmon's Quay

Corporation Staith

Kirton's Quay later Brighams Dry Docks

Slips

T.D.E. Dry Docks

Ferry still in use

The Low Graving Dock

Clive Street

Market Place

NORTH SHIELDS

Brewery

Engine Works

Duke Street

Slips

Smiths Dry Docks

Below: Harton High Staiths around 1890. Coal chauldron wagons bearing the legend *Harton* are still being led by horses to the 'drops.' Stag, a common tug, would have been taking bunker coal whilst astern, the three-masted collier brig *Aspasia* (202 GWT) is taking a full load. She was built at Bideford in 1870 for the F. Holwell shipping company, of London. Note the elaborate figurehead beneath her bowsprit. *North of England Open Air Museum, Beamish.*

1806 that we learn of the sad fate of their last (and finest) product. She was the 36-gun frigate, the *Saldanha*. Launched on December 8 1809 she was lost with nearly all her crew, including the Commander, the Hon. William Pakenham, at Lough Swilly off the coast of Ireland on December 4 1811. She had the best of material lavished upon her, and (Amy tells us) "...her loss was one of the prime factors of his downfall." It appears his reputation went down with her!

The famous Smith's Dock Company, dating from 1756, could also be found near here. This yard opened about 1850 and amalgamated with the Edwards family firm at the turn of the century to form what is the North-East's biggest ship repairing facilities...even today. Further still is the fish-quay and what North Shields

is perhaps best known for....kippers. The area was once dotted with the distinct smelling curing houses.

The high ground above the Union Quay is the site today of the Stag Line Offices with their Stag legend displayed to all passing shipping. Clifford's Fort beyond, although dating back to the 17th century was used to defend the river as recently as the Second World War and the Fort is almost in line with one of the most important safety aids to early mariners...the Low and High Lighthouses. When vessels approached from sea a safe entrance past the lurking Black Midden Rocks was assured as long as they kept the lights in line. Many, beaten by the weather, looked to the Coastguard as their last chance, sadly a great many perished.

Above: Occasionally, a passing cruise liner would anchor off the Tyne and send a boat load of tourists to the North East. Such an occasion was July 3 1971 when a 24,000-tons Holland-America cruise ship (outward bound for the USA) called to allow 160 of the passengers to visit the Roman Wall and Durham Cathedral. Here, the ship's jolly-boat is about to disembark passengers at South Shields ferry landing; keeping an eye on proceedings is the river customs launch! *South Shields Gazette.*

Left: Parents of naval cadets are treated to a tour of the harbour and a visit to the newly arrived HMS *Satellite*. She had recently replaced a minesweeper of the 'Algerine' class, which stood at Shields as the drill ship from 1947 to 1951. *Satellite* was formerly the minesweeper *Brave*, built at Blyth in 1943. She served in her cadet role until 1958 when she went upriver for the last time to be broken up at Clayton & Davie at Dunston. *South Shields Gazette*.

Below: A group of children cross the river on a small motor launch. *South Shields Gazette*.

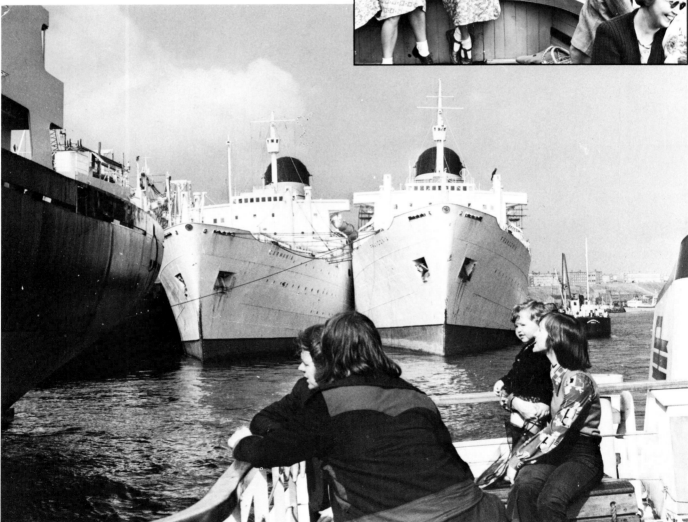

Above: A journey across the Tyne aboard the *Freda Cunningham* between the two 'Shields' was not always an easy trip, especially when ships waiting at Smiths Dock created a navigational hazard. On September 19 1973, the Cunarders *Franconia* and *Carmania* were laid up awaiting sale to Russia. Both built by John Brown's famous yard at Clydebank in the mid-1950s, they were two of four ships designed for the Canadian service from Liverpool. In 1990, this pair are still at work for the Russians. *South Shields Gazette*.

Above: A panoramic view from above Brigham Docks at South Shields. The 'Narrows' leading out to the North Sea and the long North Pier are all clearly evident. Of special interest in the centre are the two huge factory whaling ships, then owned by Salveson's. In the middle dock is the black hulled *Southern Harvester* and outside, her sister *Southern Venturer*. As a matter of interest, they were both bought (with their whale quota) in 1963 and were broken up without further trading. Could it be that the Japanese were simply interested in the whale quotas? *South Shields Gazette.*

Above: An example of the great variety of shipping built and repaired on the Tyne. In 1982, the lightship *Varne* awaits her regular service at Smiths Dock, North Shields. *Varne* would have her flashing equipment checked by officials of Trinity House to see that her 'Red Flash' occurred every 20 seconds and was clearly visible from at least 11 miles away. *Ken Groundwater.*

Left: The Brighan & Cowan Yard of 1902 amalgamated with the neighbouring Tyne Dock Engineering Yard, and, with others, formed the NE Coast Ship Repairers Ltd. A subsequent takeover by Court Line ended in disaster when the company crashed in 1974. After receiving Government help they were nationalised as part of British Shipbuilders but the company was subsequently returned to private hands after a workers buy-out in the 1980s. Here, in 1960, and still as 'Brighams' the *Alan Evelyn* (owned by Furness Shipbuilders) receives attention and a coat of paint. In 1965 she became *Rio Azul* and later the *Loida* but reached the end of the road in 1979 at Kaohsiung. *John Johnson.*

Below: The Falklands dispute coincided with a major re-fit of HMS *Fearless* at the Middle Docks, South Shields. The work to convert her to an assault support craft took some considerable time and she set sail for the long journey along with the Vickers-built carrier *Invincible*. *Ken Groundwater.*

Above: South Shields in 1945 and a new riverside building goes up after the interruption of the war. The cleared land alongside was once the early slips of Readhead, Marshall and Rennoldson and is now unrecognisable. Behind, France Fenwick's tugs lead the brand new Swan Hunter cable ship *Monarch* out to the sea. In 1969, she was renamed *CS Monarch* and sold in 1970. Her name was then changed to *Sentinel*; the ship's last days came in October 1977 when she was towed into Blyth for breaking by Hughes Bolckow. *University of Newcastle.*

Above: A 1973 view down onto the three converging dry docks at the ship repair yard of Smiths Dock, at North Shields. A Holder Brothers ore carrier is noticeable with its distinctive Maltese Cross symbol upon the funnel. *University of Newcastle.*

Above: There's little need to introduce this location. Smiths Dock ship repairers became the biggest in the world in 1899 when they abandoned ship-managing to concentrate on repairs. Today, the company continues to thrive. This 1959 view shows from left to right the *Tiderange* (1956, Sir James Laing, Sunderland) *Angola* (1948, Hawthorn Leslie, Hebburn) and *British Princess* (1946, Wm. Doxford, Sunderland). The naval oiler *Tiderange* became *Tidesurge* in the late 1960s. *John Johnson.*

Left: One of the Pederson's sailing ships which occasionally graced our shores is seen leaving the Tyne after bringing in Swedish timber, circa 1920. The old staiths (as shown on our map) near the Groyne are still in evidence. *South Shields Library.*

Below: Recalling the days of sail on the Tyne; an unidentified three-masted schooner is led to sea by the tug *Francis Batey*. The cliffs of old Tynemouth lie behind. *South Shields Library.*

Right: *Coble Dene*, a paddle tug, was a typical example of Victorian iron shipbuilding. Few of these Tyne built tugs were retired early and the *Dene's* lifespan from 1883 to 1954 was not unusual. Built in our own South Shields Yard of Hepple & Company, she served the Tyne Improvement Commission faithfully. Her duties frequently took her into close contact with extensive timber stockpiles at Albert Edward Dock and she therefore received a cinder catcher on her smoke stack. She quietly slipped from the Tyne scene in 1954. *South Shields Library.*

Above: Many Tynesiders will remember the day in 1970 that the first super-tanker *Esso Northumbria* left the river. Thousands lined the banks of the Tyne from Wallsend to the Piers to see this huge ship float out, possibly never to return. At 126,543 tons, she took Swan Hunter over a year to complete and was the first of six similar vessels. Her type was to be the economic answer to survival when the orders were thin. But things went wrong – not so much for the builders but for their owners. Oil demand and prices slumped and her steam turbines were expensive to maintain whilst idle. Construction of massive ships like this reawakened Geordie pride in things maritime, after a long period of unspectacular work. *Trevor Ermel.*

Above: We must not forget the work of the tiny pilot cutters, for these small but important boats are responsible for guiding ships into the river. Their work is extremely dangerous and entails the utmost skill. All passenger ships are required by law to take on pilots when entering the Tyne - other ships have an option. This pilot boat was the *Caer Urfa* and is seen in 1960. *John Johnson.*

Above: Perhaps not something to dwell upon, but the mouth of the Tyne has seen more than its fair share of maritime disasters. On January 20 1963, the *Adelfotis II* was outward bound from the River Tees to a Scottish port when steering problems forced her to come into the Tyne for attention. In an easterly gale, with heavy seas, she ran onto the south side of the Groyne at South Shields and all 23 of her crew were taken off by breeches buoy (as seen here) by the South Shields and Sunderland Life Brigade. She remained beached, until a scrap dealer dismantled her late in the year. *South Shields Library.*

"LINERTON," OF NEWCASTLE.
9TH NOV. 1919.
IN FOREGROUND REMAINS OF
"CONSTANCE ELLEN"
12TH NOV. 1901.

Above: The *Linerton* of 1919 was built by Doxfords on the Wear for R. Chapman & Son of Newcastle. One of three sisters, she sailed on her maiden voyage from the Tyne November 4 that year but just off the river, she suffered a serious engine failure and eventually drifted ashore at South Shields. With her back broken, both sections were refloated and taken to Rotterdam for reassembly as the tanker Radix for the Anglo Saxon Petroleum Company. She foundered and was lost October 19 1944 by which time she was known as the *Juan Casiano*.
South Shields Library.

ACKNOWLEDGEMENTS

My thanks to George Scott, for lending his time and knowledge so freely; Paul Hood, for introducing World Ship Society Members; Roger Woodcock, Ian Rae (and Swan Hunter) John Proud, Joe French, Tony Smith, Cliff Parsons and John Johnson for researching their respective photographic material; Keith Byass and Laurence Dunn for printing late into the night! For information received I wish to thank Tony Wickens, Phil Atkins, Joe Clarke, Norman McCord and Doug Kinghorn.

Special thanks also to the staff at South Shields Library and their local studies librarian Keith Bardwell. At Newcastle Library, Frank Manders and his staff were, as ever, patient beyond belief. Thanks to the staff at the South Shields Gazette for the extended loan of several prints and finally Eileen Carnaffin at Gateshead Library Local Studies for knowing where everything is!

Bob Laidlaw drew the river maps with fine attention to detail and made useful suggestions towards presentation.

Finally, my thanks to my wife, Pauline, who exchanged a hot ironing board for a hot keyboard and typed the manuscript.

BIBLIOGRAPHY

Coals from Newcastle by Roger Finch.

The Making of the Tyne by R.W. Johnson.

Charles Mitchell, (Victorian Shipbuilder) by D.F. McGuire.

Power on Land & Sea (R&W Hawthorn Leslie) by Joe Clarke.

A History of Newcastle upon Tyne by R.J. Charleton.

The History of Shipbuilding in South Shields (Notes) by Amy Flagg.

University of Newcastle; Archive Teaching Units, *The Tyne* and *Gas & Electricity Colliers,* by D R Chesterton & R.S.Fenton (WSS)

The Shipwrights by David Dougan

Many entertaining '*Waterfront*' articles by Shields Gazette.